BE[T...]
T/
SUPPORT AND HARD WORK!
JAMES 1:5
PASTOR DON

Ed's Tohlet
AND OTHER STORIES

Don Keele, Jr.

TEACH Services, Inc.
P U B L I S H I N G
www.TEACHServices.com • (800) 367-1844

Copyright © 2016 TEACH Services, Inc.
Copyright © 2016 Don Keele, Jr.

ISBN-13: 978-1-4796-0676-4 (Paperback)
ISBN-13: 978-1-5725-0677-1 (ePub)
ISBN-13: 978-1-4796-0678-8 (Mobi)

Library of Congress Control Number: 2016905573

Published by

TEACH Services, Inc.
PUBLISHING
www.TEACHServices.com • (800) 367-1844

CHAPTER OVERVIEW

- *The Bible is the Word of God, not a rulebook, but a roadmap for your life.*
- *Jesus is the One who never changes in a universe that always does.*
- *God keeps a family album, and your picture is in it.*
- *God's plan for you is life as He lives it.*
- *There is in the heart of God a place you can know as home.*

Sometimes the only way through is a miracle. God is still a God of miracles.

What happens when the miracle you pray for doesn't come through? How to hold on when life doesn't go the way you think it should.

CHAPTER 1

Smells

Smells. They are enough to cause your mouth to water or your stomach to turn. While some smells can transport us in our mind to our favorite place, other smells are just downright nauseating. And have you ever noticed how smell conscious we've become as a society?

We judge a lot of things by the way they smell. Fruit. Vegetables. Leftovers. Service-station restrooms. The kid who sits three rows over in Algebra. Mothers can even pass judgment on their teenager's room with a statement about smell. "Clean up this room! It looks like a bomb went off in here and smells like a pigsty."

There are smells just about everyone loves. Fresh-baked bread. Fresh air after a spring rain. The smell of new leather. Likewise, there are smells that almost everyone hates. Skunk spray. The inside of a garbage truck. A dirty, wet dog. Now that's nasty!

I remember the first time I really became aware of my smell-consciousness. Sometime during the summer of 1972 my dad came home and asked us if we were interested in going to visit his sister and her family for Christmas. He told us that my grandparents, as well as his other sister and brother, were going to be there and wanted us to join them.

Now that doesn't sound so unusual, except that my aunt and uncle were missionaries in Haiti. They lived on a beautiful campus right outside Port-au-Prince. This would be a perfect chance to see the "missionaries and colporteurs across the sea" that we prayed for every night, up close and personal. If we were going to go, Dad informed us, we would need to start saving our money. We were enthusiastically up to the adventure, so we started saving.

We had garage sales, took stuff to sell at the local flea market, cut our expenses, and started putting the savings into a fund for our trip to Haiti. The plan was to have a big family Christmas in Haiti.

My dad was the oldest of his siblings. The funny thing is that his youngest brother, my Uncle Rodney, came as a complete surprise to my grandparents and was only six months older than me. This particular Christmas, he would turn fifteen, while I would remain six months behind at fourteen. But we were teenagers nonetheless, and we knew everything, so there was nothing we couldn't handle. Or so we thought.

Christmas break finally came, and we packed the car and headed for Florida. Meeting the relatives in Miami, Florida, we all boarded a flight bound for Haiti. Our adventure was in full swing.

The country of Haiti shares an island with another country, the Dominican Republic. Final approach to the runway was over the water, and as we came in just above the waves, I thought we had come to paradise. The ocean water was a clear, beautiful, turquoise blue. Looking down, I could see twenty or thirty feet down into the water. I could even make out a few of the larger fish. This was going to be an amazing Christmas.

My aunt and uncle and their four children were there to meet us at the airport with two vans from the mission compound. After clearing customs and exchanging happy hugs and laughter, we loaded our baggage into the vans and headed out of town to their house. I was to learn, on the short ride home, that Haiti is actually one of the poorest countries in the world.

We passed little tin shacks with no floors and dirty little children with no clothes. We passed a corner where deformed children sat begging. Arms bent at weird angles, twisted legs, and hollow staring eyes reflecting little hope of life changing for them. My heart went out to them.

As we moved on through the city of Port-au-Prince, what really caught my attention were the smells. Mostly bad. They had a way of taking my breath away. Smells inundated me from all sides. I was immersed in a world of smells. Smells that I had never experienced before. Smells I liked. Smells that made me want to throw up. Which brings me back to two teenaged boys and our belief that there was nothing we couldn't handle.

About eight days into our stay, we were feeling pretty confident about our ability to navigate the city on our own, having grown used to the smells and sights surrounding us. We were downtown with everyone and had just finished eating lunch, when we decided it was time to make our move. We begged our parents to let us go exploring alone. After conferring with my missionary uncle, they decided it would be safe enough for us to explore on our own for a few hours. Following the usual parental warnings and agreeing to meet them at the waterfront markets by dark, we were ready to head out.

"Hey, guys," Uncle Allen called to us as we were walking off, "if something happens, do you know how to get back home?"

"No," we answered sheepishly.

"To get home, you will need to head over toward that tall building. Just on the other side of the building is the street that runs past the mission campus. Once you get to that street, find a 'tap-tap' [Haitian taxi] that is going in the direction of those hills." He pointed. "Then, as one approaches just hiss like this—*sssssssssssssssssssssssssss*," he demonstrated. "They will pull over, and you get in. When you get to the mission, pull the rope that runs along the ceiling and a red light will come on the dash and the driver will stop. Give him one of these each," he said as he handed us one coin each. "That's called a gourde. It's worth about $.20 US cents, but that will cover your ride home. Don't spend it, or you will have an angry driver on your hands."

"Do they really stop if you just hiss?" I asked, thinking that he must be trying to pull one over on us.

Without saying a word, he turned toward the street as a "tap-tap" approached.

"*Sssssssssssssssssssssssssss*," he hissed.

Without hesitation, the driver swerved toward the curb. My uncle leaned in the window and said something in the native Creole language. The driver laughed, waved, and sped away. Uncle Allen then turned back to us.

"Do you believe me now?" he asked. We nodded. "Good!" he grinned, "So go and have fun. Just don't spend that coin. And stay away from the meat market part of town."

At that time Port-au-Prince was a fairly safe city, with one exception. The meat market. All week we had heard stories of the meat market from some of the local kids who were friends with my cousins. Scary stories. Stories so bizarre that we didn't know whether to believe them or not.

According to these tales, there was a hidden trap door behind the counter. The common thread in all of the stories was that unsuspecting kids from out of town or out of the country would be lured in behind one of the meat counters to their doom. Down through the trap door they would go, and according to some of the storytellers, the next day they themselves would be the meat special.

It was enough to make you shudder one of those deep shudders that makes the hair on the back of your neck stand up and breakdance.

And, of course, any telling of the story was always accompanied by the warning not to go to the meat market by ourselves. Checking the stories with my uncle had simply brought the response that he didn't know how accurate they were, but that it was known to be a bad part of town that was best avoided.

So, once free of parental control, we naturally headed directly for the meat market—and a whole new load of smells. In the 90+ degree Fahrenheit heat, the smells were at best, stifling and at worst, downright nauseating. Meat hung everywhere from hooks in the 2x4's nailed overhead. No refrigeration. Nothing to protect it from the mass of flies that crawled all over the now-rotting carcasses.

A lady asked to see a particular side of beef. The butcher simply waved his hand in front of it, and the hoard of flies lifted off, revealing the meat underneath. She decided that was the one she wanted. I inwardly wretched.

"Hey, you. Boy." A voice sounded behind me. I spun around to see another butcher calling out to me. "Do you want to come and see today's special?" he called out. "Come on back here—I'll show you something special."

I looked around for Rodney. He was about ten feet away but had also heard the invitation. He raced over to me and grabbed my arm and said, "Let's get out of here."

"Do you want to come and see today's special?" he called out. "Come on back here—I'll show you something special."

We took off running with a Haitian butcher yelling for us to come back and "see the special." We ran about three or four blocks before we stopped. It was then that we discovered a new problem. We had no idea where we were.

We decided that we would head toward the ocean and the waterfront markets, but we soon found ourselves deeper in the wrong part of town. Suddenly, a strong arm grabbed mine. I looked up into the face of a large Haitian man who began dragging me on one side and Rodney on the other toward this dark, run-down building.

"Hey," I yelled. "What are you doing?"

"They pay me to bring you in for good time" was his only response.

"Who paid you?" Rodney asked.

He only motioned toward a building with his head. We

looked the direction he motioned to see three women and a couple of rough men watching us closely.

"How much did they pay you?" Rodney quickly asked.

"One gourde."

Rodney rapidly jerked out the coin my uncle had handed him and motioned for me to do likewise. "Here's two gourdes to let us go."

"OK," he said, quickly releasing us, grabbing the coins, and bolting away from the building. We took off running the other direction as the five people on the porch jumped up and began yelling.

After about three blocks, we slowed to a walk, trying to catch our breath and looking behind us to make sure no one was following.

"I don't know about you," Rodney spoke, "but I've about had all the excitement I can stand. It's too hot!"

I looked at my watch. Only forty-five minutes into our grand adventure and I had to admit that I was ready to head back to the mission compound as well. We turned and looked for the tallest building only to find that we had run way past it in our rush to get away. But, we reasoned, if we just turned right at the next street and went up about four or five blocks we should intersect that street and get a "tap-tap" headed toward the hills and enjoy the ride home.

We turned right onto the next street, a dirt one, and headed up the block. As we walked, we discussed our close calls and wondered aloud what other adventures might await someone in this part of the city. We didn't have long to wonder. So absorbed in our conversation, we hadn't noticed the dirt turning to a sloppy mud until we found ourselves deep in the middle of it. Suddenly our senses were jerked back to the present. With each step, our feet sunk down about three to four inches into the dark mire. The smell was overwhelming and flies buzzed all around us.

Looking toward either side of the street, we noticed that the outer edge of both sidewalks was lined with about an eight-foot plywood wall, open only about fifteen inches up at the bottom. It was then that we realized we were smack in the middle of one of the city's public restroom streets.

Haitians began peeking out around the end of the plywood wall. They gave us weird looks. They laughed and pointed at the two white tourists now wading in their public sewer. A crowd gathered on both sides of the street, but since we were over halfway up the block, we decided it would be better to go forward and try to tiptoe our way on out than to go back.

No looking cool here. There was no way to even try and look cool. Oh, we were dressed like cool American teenagers of the 70s right down to our footwear. One of the current fashion trends of the day was to wear the red canvas, hi-top, Converse tennis shoes until they had big rips and holes in them. The more rips and holes you had and yet could continue to wear them, the cooler you were. Let me tell you, we both had shoes that were barely hanging in there—extremely cool by all fashion standards. But in our current situation, as the muck and mire of human waste oozed in and under and around our feet, sucking at the soles and straining at the last remaining fibers holding the rubber and canvas together, we thought they were anything but cool. So much for fashion.

Finally exiting the block, we looked frantically for a faucet sticking out of some building to wash off our feet. Not seeing any, we spied three large jars filled with water. The first was murky and nasty smelling. The second was a little better, but the third was pretty clean. We opted for that one.

"Here, Rodney," I said. "Hold your feet out, and I'll pour water on them, and then you can pour water on mine." We had just finished washing the worst off of his feet, and I had one foot halfway done when a rather angry-looking Haitian man came running at us from way down the block screaming in Creole punctuated with one word in English. "GO!"

Not totally sure who he was talking to, and certainly not understanding the language, Rodney poured a little more water on my feet. This apparently infuriated the man because he now snatched up a large, leather-sheathed machete as he continued to run toward us shouting "GO!!!" With the translation being complete in our smell-dulled minds, we quickly decided we would "GO!!!" Rodney tipped the jar back upright, and we again found ourselves with wildly rushing adrenalin and flailing limbs to match. As I ran, one shoe sloshed and squirted water out the holes, while the other stuck tight to my foot.

It wasn't long before we found ourselves on the right street, hissing like snakes on steroids at anything that moved. A "tap-tap" going our direction pulled over to the curb. We went around back and jumped in.

> **It wasn't long before we found ourselves on the right street, hissing like snakes on steroids at anything that moved.**

I must explain that a "tap-tap" is merely a Nissan or Toyota pickup truck that has been modified to act like a bus. The bed has two benches facing each other running down either side and hanging out the back by about two feet, with a brightly decorated top and side boards, leaving two- or three-inch slats in between for some exhaust-tainted air to force its way into the occupants.

Grateful to have a ride, we plopped down on one of the benches of the near-empty truck and started to relax. Within three blocks, however, we were praying we would survive the ride, for we found ourselves in the back of a wildly-bouncing, swerving, pickup in very close company with no less than eighteen Haitians. Twenty of us piled in the back of a careening, shock-starved Nissan, and the dude sitting next to me had a chicken on his lap.

Let me remind you that it was 90+ degrees Fahrenheit, with about 90 percent humidity and many Haitians in the 70s had yet to learn of personal hygiene and deodorant. Add that to our now rotting shoes, and you had a wall of stink that was almost visible. Rodney and I pressed our noses to the little slats and sucked in "fresh" air. We would hold our breath until we were turning blue, then exhale quickly while turning our heads toward the slats behind us to repeat the process, all the while desperately watching for our stop.

The thing that absolutely blew my mind was that not one of them seemed to notice the smell at all. They just bumped on down the road, laughing and talking, totally oblivious to anything that might have been out of the ordinary. We, on the other hand, continued to fight for every breath of anything but putrid air.

Our stop finally came, and we both pulled hard on the rope. The driver swerved to the side of the road and came to a screeching halt. We piled out and sucked in the sweet air now only tainted with truck exhaust. Walking around to the driver, we both produced another gourde from our unused shopping money and began trudging up the hill to our uncle's house on the compound, covered in smells we greatly wanted to lose.

Which brings me to a question. If God could open your spiritual nose, how would your soul smell? Have you stopped to ponder lately the condition of your own soul? Are you just bumping along on life's road oblivious to the sin in your life that may be causing a stench in the nostrils of God?

Oh, I know it's not your intent to smell bad spiritually. I know you don't want God to be holding His nose over you, gasping for whatever bit of clean air He can find. But it happens. It happens through not taking care of our spiritual cleansing needs. It also happens through straight-up rebelling. Listen to what God said about His people in the days of Isaiah the prophet.

All day long I have held out my hands to an obstinate people, who walk in ways not good, pursuing their own imaginations—a people who continually provoke me to my very face, offering sacrifices in gardens and burning incense on altars of brick; who sit among the graves and spend their nights keeping secret vigil; who eat the flesh of pigs, and whose pots hold broth of impure meat; who say, "Keep away; don't come near me for I am too sacred for you!" Such people are

smoke in my nostrils, a fire that keeps burning all
day. (Isa. 65:2–5)

Did you catch that? People who are obstinate, people who
walk in their own ways, pursuing their own imaginations,
are people who continually provoke God to His face. That's
hardcore! He goes on to say, "Such people are smoke in my
nostrils, a fire that keeps burning all day."

Like acrid smoke that keeps following you at a campfire,
burning your eyes and nose, are your sins to God. If you live
outside of a relationship with God, the Bible says the smells
of your soul burn God's nose. But it doesn't have to be that
way. God has provided a way to lose the smell of your soul.
The apostle John gives us the key. "If we confess our sins, he
is faithful and just and will forgive us our sins and purify us
from all unrighteousness" (1 John 1:9).

God, Himself, will do the work. He'll clean you up. He'll
help you start over. He'll get rid of the soul stench in your
life. As you start this book, why not determine to start over
with God right now. Pray the prayer of King David when he
was confronted with his own sin.

Wash away all my iniquity and cleanse me from
my sin. For I know my transgressions, and my sin
is always before me.... Cleanse me with hyssop, and
I will be clean; wash me, and I will be whiter than
snow.... Create in me a pure heart, O God, and renew
a steadfast spirit within me. Do not cast me from your
presence or take your Holy Spirit from me. Restore to
me the joy of your salvation and grant me a willing
spirit, to sustain me. (Ps. 51:2–12)

That's all God needs to hear, and He promises to take
your smells away. Pray that prayer, right now, and let God
get rid of the stench in your soul. And then keep reading,
because the adventure is just beginning.

CHAPTER 2

Climbing the Walls
for Guinness

Three blasts on the whistle. "All right, that's a new WORLD RECORD!!! Everyone can come down." With that, everyone broke into spontaneous cheers, shouts, and laughter followed by a series of high five's after we had reached the floor. We had done it! We had set a new world record for wall climbing for the *Guinness Book of World Records*!

Our search for the title had begun only a week before when I was sitting in my dorm room. Jim, the resident assistant for my hall on the third floor, had noticed that I was having a hard time making the transition from high school to college. Having heard from my older sister that I loved to try zany things, he walked in this particular night and dropped an open copy of *Time* magazine onto my lap.

"So whaddaya think?" Jim asked. "Do you think we can beat that?"

I looked at the photograph of sixty-nine Princeton students who had just set a new world record for wall climbing. The caption under it read, "School life drives these students to climb the walls for a new world record." The picture showed some of the guys back to back, with their feet on the walls.

Some, who were tall enough, were stretched out with hands on one wall, and feet on the other. The one thing they all had in common was that all of them were off the floor.

My mind went into overdrive. Not only did I think we could beat it, but I believed we could smash it so soundly that mighty Princeton would be reeling at the thought of a small, southern, private college slam-dunking their record. We immediately laid plans. We would try to line it up for next Monday night. We would attempt it at 10:30 p.m. since that was dorm curfew and we had the best chance of getting the most guys. I would be in charge of gathering people. Jim would secure the dean's permission. Steve, my roommate, would contact the press to make sure we had it in the newspaper and to have adequate pictures proving we had done it. We would have every participant sign in front of a notary public to certify that we weren't lying. Then Jim would send off the entire packet of signatures, newspaper clippings, and photos to Guinness. I could sense fame already. Imagine, our picture—and record—in the book right along with the guy who swallowed 110 live goldfish.

I totally forgot about homesickness as the next week became a blur of activity all aimed at a new world record. I banged on all of the doors in the dorm and introduced both myself and "the plan." Most of the guys eagerly took hold of the idea and promised to be a part of the attempt, especially after I mentioned the goldfish man. People began talking to me in the halls about the big event. The dean even stopped me and asked how the plans were coming.

Monday night finally came and by 10:15, the third floor main hallway was filling with guys from all over the dorm. I lost track at about 200. At 10:20 the photographer and a reporter from the city newspaper arrived. At 10:25 the notary public came in, followed by all three deans, who were wearing referee shirts and whistles. (We had asked the deans to referee, blowing the signal whistle and making sure that all the guys were up off of the floor at the same time.) There was definitely an air of excitement and suspense. We were going to "blast" Princeton's record!

At 10:30 the head dean blew his whistle and announced through a battery operated megaphone that we were going to spend some time practicing, making sure we were comfortable with the position we chose, so we could hold it for three minutes. This would give the photographer a chance to get some shots from a number of different angles. We practiced.

For my part, I had chosen John to go back to back with me. John was another freshman on my hall. We pushed back against each other, locked our arms, and then placed our feet against opposite walls. We walked up about halfway. Once we were sure we could hold it, we walked back down. Just then, the dean blew his whistle signaling for silence.

We needed to count, he said, to make sure we were breaking the record, before we made any attempts. We laughed. The other two deans began counting while he continued. Also, we were allowed three chances, in case someone slipped and fell. One blast of the whistle would signal the beginning of the climb. Two blasts would indicate that everyone was up. Three would signal the end of the three minutes. The count turned up 347 guys.

He asked, "Is everybody ready?"

"YES!" we all screamed back. The excitement had reached a fevered pitch.

The whistle sounded. We climbed. The photographer snapped. The reporter scribbled. Our backs began to ache. Guys groaned as time seemed to stand still. Everyone held until finally ... three blasts on the whistle.

"All right, that's a new WORLD RECORD!!! Everyone can come down."

"All right, that's a new WORLD RECORD!!! Everyone can come down." With that, everyone broke into spontaneous cheers, shouts, and laughter followed by a series of high five's after we had reached the floor. We had done it! We had set a new world record for wall climbing for *The Guinness Book of World Records*! We all lined up to sign the notary's registry.

The next day we found our picture in the local city newspaper. Not the front page like we had hoped, but back about three pages into the Local section. There was a short story about us smashing the record. The reporter and his editor obviously didn't see it as very important, but I was proud to be part of such a momentous occasion.

Jim got a letter from Guinness about six weeks later. We opened it expectantly, only to find that our attempt was not "official" because we had not had a Guinness representative present. Besides, the letter went on to say, Princeton's record had been officially broken last week by another school up north with a record setting 612 people. One last note, Guinness was seeking to do away with some categories, as it was too time-consuming to follow up on all of the attempts. This would probably be one of the categories.

So that was it, huh? Shut out because we weren't "official." All of the effort wasted. All of the knocking on doors null and void. Oh, to be sure, I made some new friends and had some great memories. But I wasn't in the book. I hadn't asked for an official representative. I didn't know we needed one.

How is it with you? There's another Book in heaven. But there's only one way to officially get into it. You've got to have an Official Representative. All of your effort is wasted, null and void, if you don't. In John 14:6 Jesus said, "I am the way and the truth and the life. No one comes to the Father except through me."

You won't find me in Guinness, but I've got my name in the Book that counts. Who needs to climb the walls for Guinness and their goldfish anyway?

CHAPTER 3

A Beautiful Day
in the Neighborhood

Third grade was a tough year for me. Not in school. I loved my schoolwork and my teacher. It was after school where I had problems, or more specifically, the walk home after school.

We lived about a half mile from the elementary school I attended, and back in the day, if you lived within a mile or so, you were expected to get yourself to and from school, either by walking or riding your bike. Fortunately, my dad worked at the academy next to the elementary school, so he would take us to school in the morning, but getting home in the afternoon and getting our chores started was our responsibility. I say "our" because my older sister, Pam, also had to walk home after school. But she didn't walk home with me.

She was taking piano lessons at the time, and since we didn't yet have a piano, she would go to the academy to practice for thirty minutes before she walked home. I, on the other hand, would start out immediately after school to see if I could make it past a certain home before the boys who lived there arrived home. If I made it before they got home, it was a good day. But if I didn't, we played a game. It was a popular game, for them, called "Beat the Dweeb," with me, of course, always being selected to play the part of the dweeb.

It was a popular game, for them, called "Beat the Dweeb," with me, of course, always being selected to play the part of the dweeb.

You need to know that I was diagnosed with asthma almost from birth, and this being the days before good inhalers, if presented with a choice between running and breathing, I usually chose breathing. I say usually, because my tormentors could almost always force me to choose "run now, breathe later," as an option. It was not a pretty sight.

A little background. They lived in a house on the corner across the road from our town's large water tower. It sat on a grassy knoll at the top of the hill with the road making a 90-degree right turn just past it and then going downhill to where I lived. To get past their house, I had three options: 1) Stay on the road all the way around the corner, the "long way"; 2) cut up and across the grassy knoll, which was the shortest route on the 90-degree corner; or 3) turn off early, go down these nice, little old ladies' driveway, cut through the woods behind the water tower and into the backyard and down the driveway of a crotchety old man who seemed to love nothing more than shooting buckshot and salt pellets at the feet of anyone who came on his property, slowly aiming further up their body if the desired results were not accomplished in a timely manner. I really never considered this to be a good option.

Back to "Beat the Dweeb." The game all started when one of them was picking on me at school one day, and the teacher heard me say "OWW ... STOP IT!" She asked what was going on, so I told her. She asked me who started it, and I simply shrugged and pointed at the source of my agitation. He, in turn, pointed at me. Since he had been in trouble for picking on people before (almost daily), she called him down and he had to stay after school. The next day he and his brother started this new game.

Here's how the game was played. They would run home across the fields the back way while I walked the road. (See running and breathing comments above.) I tried to walk fast in hopes of beating them, but I rarely did. They would hide somewhere in their yard, the trees, or over by the water tower so that I had no clue where they might be coming from. Once in position, they would wait for me to try and sneak past. Then, at a given signal, they would run or drop from their hiding places, screaming and running toward me. One of them would knock me down, and then they would take turns kicking me or beating on me, calling me names like "Little Snitch" or "Sissy" or "Girl" or "Dweeb" (hence the name I gave the game). The game would go on until they got tired or felt like they had expended as much energy as they could afford for the day; then they would run off laughing. When it first started, I tried to fight them, but found I was too small, too weak, too winded, as well as outnumbered, and soon reverted to just balling up and covering my head and just waiting it out. Once they were done, I would uncover my head slowly, to make sure they were gone, and then get up and head for home.

There were a few variations to the game. As they got better at chasing me, instead of just knocking me down or tripping me, they added a new challenge for themselves. They would run alongside me and try to grab one of my fleeing feet and then jerk it out from underneath me, causing me to tumble, before allowing the game to proceed normally from there. My only hope was to get over the crest of the hill by the water tower and in sight of the home on the downhill side of the tower. If I could get that far before they caught me, the lady who lived there would often come out and rescue me, with them running as soon as her front door opened.

She would dust me off and ask me if I was all right. Being totally humiliated, I would assure her that I was and then ask her please not to tell my parents or anyone about it. I told her that I knew it wouldn't last much longer. I would then go home and change clothes, putting my dirty, grass-stained clothes in the washer and get them started before starting any of my other chores. Usually by the time the clothes were done washing, my sister would come in and start her chores, and since I was now in my "work clothes" she would be none the wiser.

Any bruises or cuts that showed up on my body I passed off as having happened by accident on the playground. I had fallen. I had slipped out of a swing. I had tripped and run into a tree. All of these were believable because of my well-known lack of athletic ability. Clumsiness, it was called in those days. As in, "that poor boy is just about as clumsy as an ox." I knew nothing of oxen and their clumsiness, just that I was often compared to them, which gave me a good alibi when it came to explaining the humiliating cuts and bruises I had received during the most recent "Beat the Dweeb" game.

One particular day the game went on much longer than normal. Perhaps the score was tied between my two tormentors and they were forced into extra innings. It could also have had something to do with the fact that I shot my mouth off to them on the playground earlier in the day when I was surrounded by my friends and feeling a little more cocky. Whatever the case, I was really catching it that day. When they finally tired and the last kick was delivered to my side, one said, "Come on, let's go," and they left.

I stiffly got up and headed home, trying to stay out of sight of any of the neighbors. I ached all over, and I cried quietly to myself as I went down the hill to the house. Once inside my bedroom, I plopped down across my bed and lay there in a pool of humiliation mixed with rage and self-pity. I wanted to get those boys so badly. I lay there for a few moments, allowing myself an anger fantasy that had me doing all sorts of things to my tormentors until they were begging me for mercy. A slamming front door brought me back to reality.

I jumped up and started to change shirts. Halfway up with my shirt, with dirt and grass in my hair and on my clothes my bedroom door came flying open. It was Pam starting to tell me about something that had happened at school. She stopped in mid-sentence, staring at the bruises on my back and my sides and the grass and dirt all over me. I pulled my shirt back down.

"What happened to you?" she asked.

"I fell off the swings at the playground," I stammered, trying to sound convincing. She looked like she wasn't buying it, so I quickly added, "I was trying to go really high and then jump out like the eighth graders do, only I messed up and ended up crashing."

She looked long and hard at me and then said, "You're lying! What really happened?"

"That's it. That's what happened," I shot back, "now will you get out of my room?"

"I'm not leaving until you tell me what really happened." She took a step forward. Though only a year older, she had already achieved her growth spurt and now towered over me. I started to leave so she grabbed me by the front of the shirt and said, "Tell me what happened."

I started crying as I jerked her hands off of my shirt, "I don't want to talk about it, now just go and leave me alone."

"Somebody beat you up. Tell me who it is and I'll take care of them for you!" she said.

This was a new ray of hope in what had become my dim existence. My sister was already well known at our school for her fighting prowess due to her go-around with the toughest school bully. He had openly challenged her in front of other kids and then thrown down the gauntlet.

She had told him, "I don't want to fight you, but don't think I can't take care of myself if you try something."

He had circled around her a few times, she turning with him, always keeping him in front of her. Finally, he had lunged in to grab her and faster than any of us knew what happened, she picked him up, flipped him over, and pile-drove his head into the grass. He lay there for a few stunned seconds, then jumped up and ran off crying, his reign of tyranny having just come to a humiliating end by no less than a girl.

I hadn't counted on Pam coming to my rescue. Perhaps it *would be* possible to end this game of "Beat the Dweeb." Maybe even forever. I turned around to face her.

"Would you really take care of them for me?" I asked.

"Sure, just tell me who they are and I'll deal with them," she responded.

I spilled the whole sordid story of humiliation and fear with them jumping out from different places and of being tripped and kicked and beaten and dirty clothes and washing them myself and not wanting anyone to know because I was embarrassed that I couldn't take care of myself.

She listened sympathetically and finally said, "OK, I have a plan." I felt better already. "Since they come out from a place you're not expecting, we're going to do the same thing."

"What do you mean by that?" I asked.

"They do the unexpected. You do the unexpected," she replied.

"I still don't get it," I said. "All I have ever been able to do is run, fall, cover my head, and endure the beating while trying to breathe. They will expect that. *I* expect that! So how am I going to do the unexpected?"

"OK, first, you aren't going to go home at the same time. You'll wait until I'm finished practicing the piano. They will be expecting you much earlier. Maybe they will get tired of waiting and then you can slip past." I liked the sound of that. She continued. "But I doubt it. So, instead of taking the road or the path over the rise by the tower, you're going to go down the path behind the trees toward the old man's house."

"What?" I cried out in shock and dismay. "No way! If I outrun them, I'll just be facing buckshot from a double-barrel."

"That's just it," she explained. "It's not what they would expect. And anyway, you're not going to go as far as the old man's place. Just toward it. Not running. Walking."

"Walking???" I shouted. "Why walking? They'll catch me sooner."

"That's the point," she said. "Don't you get it? You're going to be my decoy to lure them behind the trees."

"What's a decoy? I don't like going behind the trees because they can beat on me longer and no one sees them."

"Precisely!" Pam said. "That gives us the advantage." Light suddenly dawned in my fogged "dweeb" brain.

"Oooohhhh, so I lead them back behind the trees, and then you can come and take care of them where no one sees. Right?"

"Exactly," she said, glad that I was finally catching on. "You lead them down the path and let them catch you." I was starting to warm to the idea when another thought hit me.

"But if they catch me, they will beat on me like before. I don't like this idea."

Pam quickly responded, "I'll take it from there, and I don't think they will want to beat on you again once I get finished with them. What do you think?"

I thought it over and said, "OK, just don't let them beat on me very long."

"I won't," she assured me. "We'll do it tomorrow."

I went to sleep that night excited that my after-school "game" might soon be over.

The next day I waited while she practiced. Then we headed home. As we neared the water tower corner, Pam turned to me and said, "OK, we don't want them to see me, so you go up and walk calmly back behind the trees. Let them see you and let them catch you. Remember, walk calmly."

"OK," I replied, "but remember, don't let them beat on me very long."

"I won't … now go." She pushed me forward.

I walked up toward the corner scanning the trees, the bushes, their yard, all around their house and finally spotted them creeping up behind their hedge. I turned into the little old lady's driveway and headed for the path through the woods. Suddenly they broke out from behind the hedge and crossed the street, screaming like banshees.

Instantly my reflexes took over. Forget walking calmly; I was out of there. They caught me just before I entered the path in the woods, but well out of site behind the trees.

"Thought you were going to sneak by us, did you?" the older one yelled as he kicked my side. "Well, think again, you little sissy."

"Yeah," said his younger brother, dropping down on top of me, grabbing me by the hair and yanking my head up. "Dumb move, dweeb. You're back here behind the trees where no one can see, so you're really going to get it today!" He slammed my head to the ground.

Come on, Pam, where are you? I thought. *Ugh. Another body slam.* Suddenly I felt both boys being lifted off of me. I rolled over slightly to see Pam, who now had each boy by the back of his shirt.

"You leave my brother alone," she screamed, as she grabbed their heads and cracked them together. *Bam!* She threw the younger one down and backhanded the older one. *Biff.* He went spinning off. The younger brother came charging in to give her a head-butt. She sidestepped him and brought both her clasped hands down onto the back of his head, sending him face first into the dirt. He began to cry and got up to run for home. The older brother was up and took a swing at her, his punch catching her firmly on the jaw. Big mistake.

She yelped, grabbed him by the shirt with her right hand and swung him into a near-perfect left jab to the nose. Blood spurted from his nose and he began to retreat toward home. She followed and pushed them both down yelling, "You touch my brother again and it will be twice as bad. I'll hunt you down if I have to. Now get on home and leave him alone. For GOOD!"

She came back over to where I lay on the ground, still very much stunned at what had just happened. She reached down and extended a hand.

"You okay?" she asked pulling me to my feet. I nodded.

"Wow—that was *awesome!*" I said. "They didn't know what hit them. You were all over them. They didn't stand a chance. Thanks."

"No problem," she said. "Let's get on home and get our chores done before Mom and Dad get home."

The next day, I again waited for Pam to finish practicing, and then I walked past their house with confidence. We went the long way around the corner. I gave them a nod and a wave as I motioned toward Pam with a look that said, "Hey, guys, you can't touch this! Got my big sister with me and you *know* she can take you both." They just sat there and watched us go by. It was, indeed, a beautiful day in the neighborhood for me.

After that, I started playing trumpet and practiced in the music building while Pam practiced the piano. We would walk home together, and as long as I was with her, all was well.

You have probably realized by now that you also have an enemy. The Bible says his name is Satan. He lies in wait just to play "Beat the Dweeb," and you're it. He comes at you from all sides. He'll drop into your head screaming what a loser you are. He'll jump out from behind the hedge and cause you to fall into the sin that so easily besets you. He'll beat you up with a well-placed punch to the heart and leave you bruised and shaking with the dirt of sin and shame all over you. He'll double you over with guilt. He will humiliate you and terrorize you. He'll cause you to be anxious during the day and lose sleep at night wondering what is coming at you next. In short, he's not a nice guy.

> You have probably realized by now that you also have an enemy. The Bible says his name is Satan. He lies in wait just to play "Beat the Dweeb," and you're it.

The apostle Peter put it this way: "Be alert and of sober mind. Your enemy the devil prowls around like a roaring lion looking for someone to devour" (1 Peter 5:8).

He's out there waiting. Lurking. Prowling. Looking for someone to devour. You. Me. Anyone he can get his demonic paws on. He's always there and always bigger and meaner than you or me. And while that's real and that's scary, here's the real deal.

We've got a Big Brother who has *already beaten him and all of his minions.* He has already cast them out of heaven, and then He came down here and continued to chase them. Satan landed a well-placed punch when he put Jesus on the cross. But the Bible says that was only a heel wound. Jesus came back from the grave and crushed Satan's head. (See Gen. 3:15.)

When Jesus died and then rose again, He beat the devil. He took command of this world and sent the devil running.

And because of that, if you walk with Jesus through the neighborhood, you need not fear Satan again. You have the authority of your Big Brother Jesus to stand on. You *can* resist Satan by calling on Jesus.

If Satan starts bothering you, all you have to do is yell, "Jesus, Satan is pickin' on me again. Can you take care of things?"

Jesus stands up in your behalf and the Bible says the devil flees. Look at scripture. "Submit yourselves, then, to God. Resist the devil, and he will flee from you" (James 4:7).

You don't have to get beat up by the devil anymore. Resist him. Not in your strength, or you'll get clobbered. Resist him by calling on Jesus. Here's how Peter finishes the thought. "And the God of all grace, who called you to his eternal glory in Christ, after you have suffered a little while, will himself restore you and make you strong, firm and steadfast. To him be the power for ever and ever. Amen" (1 Peter 5:10, 11).

CHAPTER 4

Secret Weapon

I've always had the athletic ability of tree bark. I'm the type that can't walk and chew gum at the same time. I've even been known to pull over to the side of the road to honk the horn. Athletics and me just don't mix.

I learned this early on when I realized, as I mentioned in the last chapter, that due to asthma, if I had to choose between running and breathing, I would usually choose breathing every time, which left me with little time to develop my athletic prowess. Nowhere was this truer than at recess. While I enjoyed the break from studies, I hated the pressure of recess, especially in the fourth grade.

Our teacher, Miss Lester, thought it important that all children learned to play together, so almost every day, she would say in her unique nasally way, "Children, line up on the line." I hated those words because I knew what was coming next. "The line" was just on the edge of the blacktop, and it is where all teams were chosen for whatever game we would be playing that day at recess. She would then continue.

"Vance, Bobby, you be our captains today." Vance and Bobby were *always* our captains, because they were the most athletic in our class. And the ritual, no matter what sport we played, was always the same.

"Bobby, it's your turn to choose first today." Bobby would then select the next best athlete in the class, and then Vance would choose the third best while Bobby and his first pick talked over who to pick next. No matter how it started, every day it ended the same. Everyone else would be picked, and I would still be standing on the line, kicking at a small rock, or uneasily shifting from foot to foot until we could be past the dreaded words that I always knew were coming. It didn't matter who had last pick, it always went something like this.

"We'll give you two girls if you take Keele too."

"No way, we had him yesterday! It's your turn to have him."

"Well, we don't want him; he can't do anything right."

"Well, it's your turn to have him, so let's get this game started."

"No wait, what if we gave you three girls?"

At which point Miss Lester would finally intervene. "Vance, it's your pick, and there is still one person, so Donnie, you are on Vance's team today." A gigantic groan would emanate from all of Vance's teammates, and someone would utter the words I least liked to hear; "Oh, great, now he'll make us lose."

I'm not sure how I could do that because I always thought it took a whole team to win or lose, but somehow they were convinced that I was the key to winning or losing. And since they were convinced, I rapidly became persuaded as well. I came to believe that I truly was the weak link on any team. Which is why my becoming a secret weapon on any sports team was so unusual. Fast forward to my junior year in academy.

My dad became principal of Thunderbird Adventist Academy in Scottsdale, Arizona, the summer before my junior year. Dad was a competitive sportsman and a good athlete despite his large frame. Ask anyone who caught his fast-pitch softball or tried to defend against him in basketball or who stepped on the racquetball court with him. Dad had a drive to win. My younger brother, Rusty, inherited that gift of athletics. I inherited other gifts, but athletics wasn't one of them. Nonetheless, Dad wanted me to get out there and try whatever sport might be going on at the time. It was time for basketball that year, and Dad pleaded with me to sign up to be selected for an intramural team.

"Why don't you try it, son? Just sign up," Dad suggested.

"I can't run and breathe at the same time." I shot back.

"Now that you have an inhaler, you can't really use that as an excuse anymore," Dad responded. "So why don't you sign up?"

"Because I'm no good at basketball, Dad, that's why. Besides, I hate the sport. Every time I mess up, some jock gets in my face and tells me what a dumb move I just made and how stupid I am for making it."

"But this is a new school. You can make a fresh start here!" Dad insisted.

"Too late for that, Dad. They've already seen me in PE class and know that I'm as coordinated as concrete. I hate the pressure, and I freeze every time someone throws me the ball. Then someone steals the ball and the rest of my team yells at me. No thanks."

He continued to plead until finally, just to please him, I signed up. Not that I was real worried that I would actually have to play. In our school, there was an "A-league," a "B-league," and a "C-league." A-league players were the best in the school. They lived, ate, and breathed basketball. B-league guys were OK, but not outstanding. And C-league ... let's just say they were the leftovers. Even at that, my skills were so poor that if there had been a "Z-league," I would have played in it. I knew, even if picked for a C-league team, that I would be adequately prepared to warm the bench. So I signed up just to get Dad off my back.

The system for choosing teams went like this. The coach would select the best of the best to be A-league captains, and

> "Too late for that, Dad. They've already seen me in PE class and know that I'm as coordinated as concrete."

they would come in the first evening and choose their teams. Then the coach would post the A-league list the next morning. The second day he would choose the best of those not chosen the first night, and they would become B-league captains. That evening they would take the remaining list and make their selections, and the next morning the B-league list would be posted, and the same procedure would follow for C-league on the third day.

When the A-league list was posted all over campus, the jocks would all gather to see what team they were on. They would high-five each other if they found they were on the same team or start talking smack about how they were going to deep-six the other team if they found out they were on opposing teams.

I was walking past the library on my way to the ad building just before the first bell rang when coach put up the A-league list. The jocks swarmed it like flies on a cow pie. It was disgusting. But it had nothing to do with me, so I decided to ignore it. I had two more days before I would have to start worrying.

"WHAT!?" one of the jocks suddenly shouted. "You've GOT to be kidding me! LOOK!" he said pointing to a name on the list.

"NO STINKIN' WAY!" yelled his new teammate. "What was Richard thinking?"

They take this way too seriously, I thought. *It's only a stupid game. Reminds me of elementary school.*

"Have you seen him play?" the first exclaimed, "He'll make us lose!"

Some things never change, I concluded. *They just need to grow up. Oh, well, none of my concern.*

The bell rang and doors all over campus flew open as students streamed out heading for their next class. I headed around the corner to the ad building.

Suddenly, though my feet were still walking forward, I found myself rapidly moving backward, carried by two big jocks.

"Hey," I started.

"Shut up, we've got to get to the bottom of this," one of them said.

They turned me around and plopped me down right in front of Richard. Richard was a senior, and one of the best basketball players in school. He was about 6'5" and at that height was also one of the tallest kids in school. He always carried himself with an easy air about him, and a toothpick was always hanging out of one side of his mouth.

"Richard, what were you thinking by picking Keele for our team? Have you never seen him play? He's horrible! He'll make us lose?" jock one almost shouted, his face red and his veins popping out on the side of his neck.

"What?" I exclaimed as the words wormed their way into my understanding. "You picked me on your team? Why?"

"That's what we want to know!" jock two jumped in. "What in the world were you thinking? Oh, you weren't!" Richard just kind of grinned and chewed on his toothpick.

Jock one joined back in, "Really, Richard, have you seen him play? He's got to be the worst of the worst. Go back to coach before they pick B-league and pick up someone else. Maybe Randy. He didn't get picked yet."

I was starting to panic as the reality of the situation sunk in. This could be extremely humiliating, because everyone came to watch A-league games. Almost no one came to C-league games.

"It's true, Richard," I said. "Randy would be a much better choice than me. I have been making teams lose for years now. I'm not your man. I really *am* bad! Just give me three minutes on the court, and I'll prove it to you. Get someone else while there is still time."

"He's making a lot of sense," jock two said. "Listen to him, Richard, before it's too late."

Richard deftly flicked his toothpick from one side of his mouth to the other with his tongue and then said, "No gentlemen, I want him on my team. I have a plan for him. He's going to be our secret weapon."

"WHAT???" we all cried in unison.

"That's right. I've got a plan that I think will work."

"But Richard," jock one started.

"Gentlemen, I want him on my team. I have a plan for him. He's going to be our secret weapon."

Richard looked at him and said, "Listen, I want him on the team, and he's going to be on the team—so either you accept that, or you can find another team."

I swallowed hard and decided to try one more tactic. "Look, Richard, what if I don't want to be on your team. What if I don't want to play at all? Did you ever think of that?"

"Your name was on the list," Richard said, "which means that you wanted to play. I picked you, so you will play on my team. Now listen, all of you, before we're late to class. Coach said that we could have the gym Sunday at 2 for just our team. I'll tell you what I'm thinking then. Be there Sunday at 2, dressed out and ready to play ball."

"But," I began to protest but didn't get any farther.

Richard turned and started walking toward his next class. "If you're not there, Keele," he said over his shoulder, "I will hunt you down and drag you there. So make it easy on both of us. Show up ready to play."

Jocks one and two angrily stomped off toward their next class, and I shuffled on to the ad building and Dad's office to lament this unfortunate turn of events. Dad was thrilled.

"Wow," he said after hearing my story, "A-league! Now you can show them what you've got!"

"Yeah, Dad," I responded, "which is absolutely nothing. I got nothing! And now the whole school will know, and I'll be the laughingstock of the entire student body."

Sunday came and I briefly thought of skipping, but remembering Richard's threat and knowing that he would follow through, I changed into my basketball shorts and headed to the gym. I hated my PE clothes. I was so skinny my shorts hung on by the drawstring for dear life. They were so big around my spindly legs that I could take three steps before the shorts even started to move.

Entering the gym, I quickly slouched to one of the benches to watch my new teammates as they warmed up. There was Joe, a short but very quick outside shooter. He would be playing guard, no doubt. There was Kevin, a 6'1" senior. I had seen him play both forward and guard. Then you had "Tank," a rather large, very enthusiastic forward. Tank was not his real name. It was actually John, but I had a bad habit of giving people private nicknames based on their characteristics. John was so enthusiastic in his play, he was often oblivious to anyone around him. He had run me over as I walked across the court one day, thus earning the nickname "Tank" in my mind. Eddie was another who could play forward or guard. Richard, of course, would play center, and I guessed my position to be sub after everyone had fouled out if they were really in desperate straits.

Richard saw me on the bench and said, "OK, we're all here. Have a seat guys, and I'll explain my plan."

They all sat along the bench, leaving a wide margin between them and me, which was OK with me. As it turned out I wouldn't be sitting there long anyway.

"Keele," Richard said looking my direction, "come out here." I got up and shuffled out toward the center of the court where Richard stood.

"Keele," he said, "this year you are going to be our secret weapon."

"I think you've got the wrong guy, Richard," I began, but he cut me off.

"Here's the plan," he continued. "Everyone already knows how bad you are at basketball, and by now word is out that I'm nuts. We're going to use that to our advantage." He paused. Somewhere off in the distance a cricket chirped as we all waited to hear what the plan was.

"Keele," he went on, "I'm gonna teach you how to play basketball."

"Coach already tried that and it hasn't worked yet," I said.

"I'm not finished, so just shut it," Richard responded.

Then to Joe, "Throw me the ball."

"Keele," he said, "we're gonna get real basic here, so follow me. This is a basketball."

"Yeah," I said, "we've got those in C-league."

"I said shut it," Richard replied. "How you gonna learn anything if you're always yappin'?" I shrugged.

"These," he pointed to the lines surrounding the court, "are the boundary lines." I started to let him know we had those in C-league too, but his look told me I should just keep it shut.

"Everything inside those lines is what we call inbounds," he continued. "Everything outside, we call out of bounds. To score, this ball must go through that hoop. We call that 'making a basket.'"

I stood there, somewhat embarrassed, trying to figure out the point he was trying to make with such obvious information, as my teammates just sat and snickered.

"Your first job on this team comes whenever the other team makes a basket. I want you to run over, grab the ball and take it out of bounds. Can you do that?"

I nodded.

"Let's practice. Pretend this is the other team." With that Richard shot the ball into the basket. I went over picked it up and walked out of bounds.

"Good," Richard said. "Now, watcha gonna do?"

"Throw it inbounds," I replied.

"To who?" Richard asked.

"Whom," I replied.

"What?" he asked.

"The correct word to use would be whom," I said.

"Hey," Richard shot back, "This ain't English class."

"Obviously," I responded, "or I would be doing a lot better."

"Look, just answer the question—Who you gonna throw it to?" Richard said.

"Somebody on my team," I said sarcastically. This was getting old and I failed to see the point.

"Only two people on this team will you ever throw it to," Richard instructed. "Me or Joe." I decided to pass on the English lesson. "Now," he said, "Let's try that. Joe, come out here. John, come guard him."

He shot the ball. I went and picked it up and headed out of bounds. "Tank" followed me. When I turned around, he was waving his arms frantically in my face trying to keep me from throwing the ball in. My view was limited to big, hairy armpits. Nasty.

"Come on, Keele," Richard shouted, "throw it in."

"Get this baboon with the hairy armpits out of my way and I will." I shouted back.

"That's the point, Keele," Richard said. "There will always be someone trying to keep you from throwing the ball in. If that should happen, turn your body sideways, keeping the ball away from your opponent. Simply throw it one-handed way up in the air, like you're doing a hook shot, and I'll get it. Now try that."

I turned sideways and launched it up over my head. It easily cleared John's waving arms. Richard leaped into the air and snatched it.

"See," he said, "No problem. Now watcha gonna do?"

"Come inbounds," I replied.

"And go where?" Richard asked.

"To the other end." I snapped.

"And do what?" he asked.

"I dunno," I said, "Run around and around and around until somebody throws me the ball."

"No," Richard said. "There is only one place you will go. This little painted section in the middle we call the key. You're going to run down and stand at the top of the key on the right-hand side."

"That's it?" I asked. "Just stand there?"

"No," Richard answered, "You will never just stand there. You will always have your hands up like this." He demonstrated by bringing his hands up in front of his chest, palms out, as if ready to catch the basketball. He continued, "Then always turn to follow the ball. Keep your hands up and just follow the ball with your eyes, keeping your body facing toward wherever the ball is. If it should come to you, simply turn toward the goal and launch it up somewhere in the vicinity of the basket. I'll be there to take care of it. Got it?"

"I think so," I responded.

"Good, anyone else have questions?" Richards asked the rest of the team.

"Yeah," said Tank, "I still don't get how this is going to work. Keele is still no good at basketball."

"He doesn't have to be," Richard countered. "That's the beauty of it. Because we are good at it, the other teams will be guarding us, but no one will guard Keele. So once we get the ball to him and he throws it toward the basket, I'll be able to shake my guys by going up after the ball. From there it should be easy. Get it?" We all answered back with blank stares. It was obvious that no one got it.

"OK, let's try it," Richard said. "I'll show you what I mean." Then to me, "Keele, try to get it somewhere close to the rim. That will help a whole lot. OK ... get in your places guys. Keele, hands up, follow the ball." Richard whipped the ball to Joe who threw it to Kevin. I turned and followed the ball with my hands up in front of my chest. Kevin to Tank, Tank to Richard. Suddenly, *whump*, it hit my hands like a cannon ball. I went two steps backwards.

"No, Keele," Richard called out, "once you get the ball you can't move your feet!"

I pulled on my jersey to release my chest from the collapsed position. "Well, I wasn't expecting it that hard," I countered.

"Always expect it hard," Richard said. "That way, if it is, you're ready. And if it isn't, you're also ready. OK ... let's try it again. Remember, Keele, close to the rim."

Richard to Kevin, Kevin to Joe, Joe to Tank and, *whump*, back in my hands. This time I turned and heaved it toward the basket. Like a flash out of nowhere, Richard came blazing past me, leaped into the air, grabbed the ball, and slammed it through the hoop. I stood there with my mouth open.

Whoa—that was cool! He turned and looked at the rest of us.

"Now do you get it?" he asked. We all nodded and then simultaneously broke into a spontaneous rant.

"Dude, that was awesome! Did you see that? That was so cool! There is no way to guard that! Unbelievable! Who would have thought?"

"Now do you see how Keele will be our secret weapon? If he can get it up in the air just like that, it should be no problem to take the lead."

I stood there shaking at the thought of not being a loser anymore. Maybe I did have hidden talents in basketball. Just be there in my spot with my hands up. Be ready. And if the ball came to me, heave it toward the basket. I could do this!

We tried the play over and over again. Sometimes I threw it flawlessly, other times, not so well. Richard developed contingency plans in case I messed up. Joe or Kevin would run in to help try and recover the ball in case things didn't go well. We kept at it until I was getting pretty consistent—and very tired. Some of the guys were running over to the water fountain. Richard called for a break. I slumped to a bench on the side of the gym. Richard came over.

"Good work, Keele! Now we just need to teach you how to play defense," Richard's words sent virtual cramps through my tired body.

"What do I have to do there?" I asked.

"Just run around and around and around till somebody throws you the ball," Richard grinned.

"Yeah, right!" I said, as I smiled for the first time that day.

"Actually," he said, "That's not far from the truth. I just want you to follow the ball. Get in their face and yell at whoever has it. Try to freak them into making a mistake. If they don't know it's coming, it can cause a turnover. We're going to try it on they guys in a minute. Are you game?"

"Just run to whoever has the ball and yell? That's it?" I asked.

"Well, that and wave your hands in front of them as you yell," Richard said. "OK, here's the deal. You, me, and Eddie

are going to take on Joe, John, and Kevin in a little scrimmage game. You just try that defense. If we get the ball, just
run back to your spot and get your hands up."

"OK," I said, "I'll try, but can we play half-court? I can't
keep running this way." Richard grinned and nodded.

We started into the scrimmage game and the ball went to
Tank. I ran over and yelled loudly, "WOOOOOOOW!" Tank
jumped back and Richard stole the ball, going in for an easy
layup.

"What was *that* about?" John yelled looking in my direction.

"That," Richard said, "was exactly what I wanted him to
do. And if it worked on you, it will work on a lot of guys." He
looked my direction and gave me a thumbs up.

Richard threw the ball to John. "So, you guys ready to
take on our secret weapon?"

We practiced until I couldn't yell, or for that matter, move
anymore. I dragged myself home for a shower, exhausted,
but feeling it might not be so bad after all.

Our first game came a few days later. The gym was packed
to watch the A-league guys play. They made a big deal of calling the starting five from each team. You know the drill. "And
starting at forward, and a big senior, is Kevvvvvvvvvvinnnnn-
nnn." Everyone cheered as Kevin ran out. "In the other forward
position, another senior, heeeeerrrrrrreeessssss Johnny!!!!"
The crowd again cheered as Tank trotted out and high-fived
Kevin. "Playing guard, he's short, but he's fast as lightning,
please welcome, junior Joooooooooeeeeeee!" The crowd went
nuts as Joe ran out with both hands up and high-fived both
Kevin and John. "And in the other guard position, also a
junior, for the first time in A-league—heeeeerrrrrrreeeessss
Donnie!" The crowd went totally silent as I took the first three
steps to get my shorts moving. Somewhere off in the distance
a dog barked. Then suddenly, I heard it—small at first, but
building in intensity. A snicker, then a short laugh, and before
I knew it, the whole gym erupted into laughter.

All of my loser feelings swiftly returned. Maybe I didn't
belong on the court. I was about ready to bolt for the door

in shame when I heard something else. A single clap. Then another one, quickly followed by a third. One person was clapping! I looked around and spotted my dad standing in the corner of the gymnasium, clapping for me!

Tank high-fived me and whispered, "Don't worry about it, man. They don't know you're our secret weapon. We'll call you SW for short. Just stay undercover for a little while longer." Instantly I felt better.

And immediately, when the rest of the students heard their principal (my dad) clapping, the laughing died away. The announcer continued.

"He's the captain of the team, he's a senior, playing center, let's hear it for Riiiiiiiiccchhhhhharrrrrddd!" The crowd abruptly went wild again as Richard trotted out and high-fived the rest of us.

After the other team was announced, we went out to line up for the jump ball. We had never covered the jump ball in any of our practice sessions, so I wasn't quite sure what to do. I stood out a little bit away from everyone else. No one came close to me either.

The whistle sounded, Richard out-jumped his opponent and drilled the ball straight to me. I had my hands up and caught it, but now what? Like a flash, Joe came right past me, snatching the ball and running straight toward the basket for an easy layup. Cool.

"Defense, Keele!" Richard yelled. "Let it go, boy!"

I ran down to the other end of the court and spotted the ball. Running full bore toward the guy, I shrieked, "YAAAAAAAAA!" as I lunged in, waving my hands frantically. He jumped back, startled, and tried to get a pass off. Tank was all over it, and Joe was already running downcourt. We were up by four in the first minute of the game.

They threw the ball in and brought it down. I was all over my defensive game! "Yaaaa! Wooooow, HAAAAAY! "WatchOUT!" I was having a great time waving my arms and yelling. Suddenly, we had the ball and everyone was running downcourt.

"Get in your spot, Keele!" Richard yelled. I ran to the top of the key and had my hands up just turning and following the ball. I began to feel like a real dufus when people started pointing and laughing, but I kept my hands up. *Whump.* I turned and launched it toward the goal. Perfect throw! Richard was on it in a flash and quickly slammed it through the hoop.

The loudspeakers came to life as the voice of the announcer tried to drown out the roaring crowd. "Two-points, Richard! Assist, Keele!"

I looked and my dad was going nuts! Clapping for all he was worth. "Get down here, Keele!" Richard yelled. Oh, yeah! I plunged into the melee. "YAAAA! Woohooo, HAAAAAY! "WATCHit!" I was like a hard-core squirrel on caffeine. It was the most fun I'd ever had on a basketball court.

At the end of the game, we were up by sixteen points, and I had twelve assists behind my name. I couldn't believe it. I was actually on a team that WON! And I had, beyond a doubt, contributed to the win! That was the first of many wins. As a matter of fact, we went undefeated the entire season.

To be sure, the other teams caught on to our strategy. I began to be heavily guarded. "Don't let Keele get that ball in the air!" other captains would caution their guards. So Richard showed me a few other moves. A head fake and toss out to Joe. A bounce pass under the jumping blocker to Tank. An around-the-back dump-off to Kevin. A handoff to Eddie. Always, I was in my spot. Always with my hands up, ready to get the pass.

And in the championship game, with three minutes remaining in the game, I had a slow-motion moment. We were playing against Ron's team. Ron was about equal in skill to Richard, and this particular game was hard fought. Someone on his team answered every basket we made. The game was tied. Adrenaline was running high. I was in my spot and I was open. Suddenly the ball was in my hands, and I turned and launched it toward the basket. That's when things went into slow motion.

Up, up, up went the ball. Ron and Richard both went up

at the same time to try and gain control of the ball. It continued going up, right over both of their outstretched hands. They waved, arms colliding. Beads of sweat went flying, glistening under the mercury lights. Still the ball was on its' upward arch. They swung again and missed, as it reached the apex, and then all three started their slow-motion descent together: Ron, Richard, and the ball, with a perfect slow-motion backspin. I stood there in my spot, watching it all unfold slowly before my eyes. As Ron and Richard hit the floor, the ball swished through the basket, nothing but net. It went IN! I couldn't believe it! It actually went IN!

Somewhere in the distance I heard the announcer say, "Two points, KEELE!" My dad went absolutely nuts, jumping and yelling, "Way to go, son! Good one!" I stood rooted to my spot, soaking it all in until Richard's voice jerked me back into reality.

"Get down here, Keele! We need you!" I sprinted down the court and went into the fray like a shark on a feeding frenzy. "YO! HAY! WATCHIT! LOOKOUT! YAAAAAHHOOOOOO!" I was all over the place! We got the turnover, and Joe was downcourt in a flash. Tank to Eddie. Eddie to Joe. Joe in for the layup. We were up by two. They were back downcourt and working it. Ron drove the basket, and we were tied again.

Back and forth it went. Final ten seconds. We had possession, and we were down by one because of a free throw. I was in my spot. Hands up. Turning and facing the ball at all times. Richard to Tank. Tank to Joe. Joe to Kevin. Kevin to me. I turned and started to launch, but two guys came out of nowhere to block it. I switched up and bounced it under them as Richard came zipping by on his way to the hoop. He took the pass and drove for the goal, with Ron guarding closely. Releasing the ball, it went up, hit the backboard and dropped through the hoop just as the buzzer sounded.

The whole place went nuts. Suddenly I found myself on the shoulders of my teammates as they chanted "SW, SW, SW!" My dad was pounding me on the back, yelling, "Way to go, son! Good job!"

Wow, from the loser's bench to the winner's circle. I had never been there before. It was an unbelievable feeling. I reveled in the glow as I went home that night. But I also felt a lot of gratitude for what Richard had done for me.

> **Wow, from the loser's bench to the winner's circle. I had never been there before. It was an unbelievable feeling.**

For some reason Richard had chosen me, a major loser, to be on his team. I think it was because he secretly wanted to date my sister (which didn't work). But he took a chance nonetheless. Even though I was a loser, he picked me to be on his team of winners.

And even though I had been the one they picked up off the floor and bounced around, I knew full well that I couldn't really play basketball. I had only done what Richard had taught me. He taught me how to stand at the top of the key and how to throw the ball up in the air. He taught me a head fake and a bounce pass and how to act like an idiot on defense, but if the truth were to be told, I'm still no good on a basketball court. I still can't play the game. But that didn't matter to Richard. What mattered was that I did what he asked.

My job was to be in my spot and be willing. I needed to have my hands open and ready to catch whatever was thrown. I needed to keep my eye on Richard and not worry about what everyone else was screaming at me. And when the ball came to me, I was to just heave it toward the basket and let him take care of the rest. Which brings me to you and your spiritual growth.

You may think that you are no good at this spiritual walk thing. You may still be stunned that for some reason God chose you to play on His team. He knows that you may not be the best at playing. He knows that the spiritual walk is hard. He knows that you don't feel adequate—but for some reason, He picked you. Look at what the apostle John wrote: "You did not choose me, but I chose you and appointed you so that you might go and bear fruit—fruit that will last—and so that whatever you ask in my name the Father will give you" (John 15:16).

He isn't asking that you have it all together. He isn't asking that you be the star player of the team. Just be in your spot and be willing to serve. Keep your heart open for whatever Jesus decides to throw at you. Jesus has rarely picked the most adequate or the most competent. But He has always used the most willing. Remember, it's not based on how bad you are, but rather on how good He is. Just be in your spot, with your hands up, ready to do what He asks of you. Throw it up there, and He'll take care of the rest. Paul reminds us that "he who began a good work in you will carry it on to completion" (Phil. 1:6).

It's His job to take you from a spiritual loser to a spiritual winner, and He wants to finish that work in your life. Allow Him to do that work and simply do what He asks you to do.

What's He asking you to do? God wants you to be in your spot with your hands up, and He wants you to put your heart and soul into it. "Love the Lord your God with all your heart and with all your soul and with all your mind and with all your strength" (Mark 12:30).

Question: How well have you been playing the game? Have you been pleading to get off of the team? Have you tried to stay on the bench? There is no excuse a Christian can stand on for not fulfilling the Gospel commission. It's a command of Jesus, not a suggestion. And with every command comes a promise. Check this out.

His divine power has given us everything we need for a godly life through our knowledge of him who called us by his own glory and goodness. Through these he has given us his very great and precious promises, so that through them you may participate in the divine nature, having escaped the corruption in the world caused by evil desires. (2 Peter 1:3, 4)

Did you catch that? His divine power has given us everything we need for life and godliness. He's already given you everything you need to be in the game. So get in there and get your hands up!

And you'll find, if you're faithful, that when the final game is played, and the final buzzer sounds, you'll be hoisted up onto the shoulders of angels and carried past God the Father, and there you will find Him applauding, saying, "Way to go, son! Way to go, daughter! I'm so proud of you! Not because you're the best basketball player out there, but because you're My child, and you learned to trust Me and you learned to trust My Son, Jesus, and together, we've made you a winning secret weapon in this whole great controversy."

So don't take yourself out of the game. Don't sit and whine that there are others better or more qualified than you. Don't excuse yourself because you aren't having fun or the work is hard. Stay in there and play. Hold on a little longer, because someday soon—it won't be long now—it's going to all be worth it. Hey, life is short, play hard!

CHAPTER 5

Ed's Tohlet

It was a frosty October morning. A thin dusting of snow was on the ground as we drove up "Four-Mile Holler." Along the way sat rusted, bullet-ridden shells of old cars from the 20s, 30s, and 40s. Black coal smoke came from several of the old shacks on each side of the road. It almost appeared as if we were going back in time as we drove the winding road in this rural part of Kentucky. Some of the teens with me huddled further down in their warm coats as they imagined what life must be like for the people who lived in such rundown, rickety places. We were on our way to see Ed and to work on his house as part of our ongoing Appalachian Outreach project.

Ed lived at the very back of "Four-Mile Holler." A "holler" in Eastern Kentucky is a hollow between two mountains where the runoff water has carved a path on its way down to the valley. This one was named "Four-Mile Holler" because it was exactly four miles long. We were to later find out it was also known as a "shootin' holler." A "shootin' holler" is a hollow in which a feud is still going on. This particular feud, I learned, had already lasted 126 years. Ed had seen many people die in the feud, but since he had remained neutral, he was rarely shot at, though his house did sustain some bullet wounds received while he was entertaining members of one family or the other.

As we pulled up in front of Ed's place, we began to realize that this was not going to be an easy job. His "house," to use the term loosely, sat back off the road at the confluence of two fairly large, rapidly-moving streams, one of which we would have to cross on a log that had been cut in half and laid across the creek. This particular morning it was encrusted in a layer of ice that looked wickedly dangerous as it showed every twisted warp of a log perched about eight feet above the wildly rushing creek.

My teens watched from the warmth of the van as I got a square-point shovel out of the trailer and began to slowly chip away the ice and inch my way across the treacherously uneven surface of the log. A gust of wind almost sent me plunging into the icy stream, but I held onto my shovel and braced against it. Ten long minutes of chipping and slowly inching my way across finally yielded success as I stepped out onto the other side. I relaxed. Too soon.

A giant dog leaped out of the tall weeds near the log bridge and snapped. I screamed and lept as the dog hit the end of the large logging chain restraining it. The teens, watching from the warmth and safety of the van, screamed with me, but once they realized I was still alive, began to laugh at my plight. I couldn't get back across the log bridge if I wanted, and they weren't about to come to my aid.

Fortunately for me, Ed had heard my scream and the door to the shanty jerked rapidly open. A rather large man, slightly hunched over an adjustable, dirty metal cane, limped out onto the porch.

"GIT'OWN!" he screamed. The large dog slunk back into the weeds. I didn't fully understand the language, but I was extremely glad the dog did.

"Hi!" I tried to sound cheerful despite my shaking knees and racing heart, "I'm Pastor Don. Are you Ed?"

"Thasright," Ed replied. "Lemme git sum ashes to put on

the log and tie back the dog. Make him safer." He grabbed an old steel pail filled with coal ash and hobbled down to the creek bank where I still stood rooted to the ground.

"Take 'is here and shovel it out on the log," he instructed, handing me the pail. He went and grabbed the beast and looped his chain over a large, metal stake farther back from the bridge, effectively making the landing safe. I shoveled ash across the log, and one by one the teens began spilling out of the van and making their way across.

"Can we pet your dog?" one of my students asked. I was incredulous after my near-death experience.

"Well, I reckon ya can ... jes don't turn yore back on 'im," Ed responded.

"What do you mean, Ed?" I asked.

Ed didn't reply, but bent down and rolled up his right pant leg to reveal a nasty looking six-inch scar on his calf.

"What happened?" we all asked, almost in unison.

"Well one day, I's down here afeedin' 'im, and I turnt around to git some water, and the fool dog done grapped ahold a mah leg and wunt let go fur nothing! He was agrowlin' and a shakin his haid around, 'bout to rip mah leg plumb off. Well ... I commenced to jerkin' on his jaws, an' abeatin on his haid ... but he won't let me go."

"How did you get him off?" I asked.

Ed looked up toward the side of his shack which had many old-fashioned iron objects hanging on the outside wall and said, "Ya see that big iron skillet ahangin' over there? Well I unhooked his chain and I went adraggin' 'im up there and got that ole' skillet, and I beat him on the haid till he went plumb

> **"The fool dog done grapped ahold a mah leg and wunt let go fur nothing! He was agrowlin' and a shakin his haid around, 'bout to rip mah leg plumb off."**

out! Then I jerked his jaws offamah leg and dragged 'eem back down there and hooked 'eem up. And ya know, that dog ain't been right ever since."

"Don't touch the dog, kids," I said

"Whul, that's mah liddle dog," Ed responded. "Mah big 'un, I had to lock up afore you'uns got here. Had 'em both bred special. Part Doberman, part Rottweiler, and part Pit Bull. Not many get past 'im on the bridge there. Kinda surprised *you* did." He gave a look my way, and I felt a new ripple of respect among the students.

"So, Ed, what do you need us to do for you today?" I changed the topic while the respect was fresh.

"I needja to put a new wall in mah kichun. It fell out on to mah porch about 3 year ago. C'mon on in ... all uh you'uns."

As we entered his house, the smell was almost an entity of its own. Getting past that, the next problem was finding a route through the junk. From the front door, a trail led between stacks of old junk radios, magazines, eight-track tape players, tapes, a car transmission and other assundry items, to the kitchen. Another trail led from the main trail over to a TV that played in two colors, red and offset green. Another trail went from the TV to the coal burning stove over in the corner and then from the coal burning stove back to the main trail.

In the kitchen, things weren't much better. Actually, it got worse. I did a double take as I looked at the dishes in the sink. The top ones looked alright, but as I looked deeper, I saw black and grey mold growing out from between the dishes on the bottom two-thirds of the stack.

"Ed," I asked, "How long have these dishes been in the sink?"

"Well, ah warshed 'em all fur 'bout the first 3 years after muh wife lef me. Then figerd ... ain't no one eatin' off'n these but me—so ah'll jes' warsh the ones ah need when ah need 'em."

"And how long ago did your wife leave you, Ed?"

"Les see," he scratched his head, "it's been 'bout fifteen year ago."

"WHAT? So you're saying these dishes have been in the sink for twelve YEARS?" I asked incredulously.

"Dat ud be 'bout right," he concluded proudly.

I asked him where they went when they were all clean.

He pointed to a cabinet. I opened the cabinet to find a lot of rat and mouse droppings and an old oatmeal box and a box of grits with long grey mold growing out of the side. As a matter of fact, mold abounded. I marveled. This would certainly be a place where penicillin could gain a foothold.

The back wall of the kitchen was completely gone—rotted away—with the remains lying on top of a broken down porch floor. All that was left was the screened-in walls of the porch, inside of which Ed had stapled black plastic as a shield against the cold. The floor of the porch was rotted through, and to one side of the porch, was another "bedroom." Actually, it was more of a storage area for more junk, with rotting floors.

I marshalled the troops, about fifteen high schoolers, and a couple of adult sponsors and prepared them for battle. We would clean the junk out of the living room, clean the kitchen, even washing dishes and cleaning out cupboards, and carrying out all of the garbage. We would also build a new wall into his kitchen. The porch and back half would have to wait for another day. This would probably take us all day.

Once everyone was busy, Ed had one more request. "I's wunderin', preacher, couldja do somthin' 'bout mah tohlet? It kindly peenches."

"Your what?"

"Mah tohlet. It kindly peenches."

"I'm not sure I understand what you're saying, Ed. Why don't you show me," I suggested.

He then led me around the corner to his bathroom. A whole new smell emerged. Old urine and waste smells lurched out and pierced my nose. He pointed to the toilet. A quick glance at

> **"I's wunderin', preacher, couldja do somthin' 'bout mah tohlet? It kindly peenches."**

the seat, and Ed's problem was obvious. Apparently he had slipped and fallen, and the front half of the ring had broken away from the back half and they were only joined now by pieces of plexiglass and superglue on the underside. So every time Ed would sit, it would "kindly peench" him.

Glancing around the rest of the bathroom revealed a nasty looking sink as well as a tub and shower enclosure. The tub and side walls were a deep rust color that looked to be layers thick. The glass doors were also covered in whatever it was. It was apparent that we needed to do something about that as well.

I had to ask. "Ed," I ventured, "how long has it been since you cleaned your tub?"

"Mah wife warshed it real good jes' before she left."

"You're telling me it's been fifteen years?" He nodded.

One of the adults headed to town to find a toilet seat, while I went to the back of the trailer to find some long rubber gloves and strong cleaning supplies, a few brushes, some steel wool pads, and whatever else seemed potentially helpful for the task at hand, then headed back in, looking for a teenager to redirect. In the meantime, Ed said he was tired and shuffled off to the back of the house to lay down for a nap.

Spying a student not doing anything, I called for him to follow me. I led him into the bathroom and showed him the nasty shower and tub enclosure. He swallowed hard and started turning pale. Obviously fighting back waves of nausea, he began to try to speak. Nothing came out, so he motioned for me to follow him. He ran outside. I followed.

"Pastor Don," he began, "if you want that shower cleaned"… long pause … careful thought … deep breath … "you're going to have to do it yourself, 'cause I ain't touchin' that thing!" With that, he turned and ran back to the job he was supposed to be helping with before I had called him.

OoooK, I thought to myself, *it's up to you, big guy. You've got to buck up and show them a little servant-leadership.*

I donned the heavy rubber gloves and picked up my cleaning supplies. This was do or die. Put up or shut up. I headed in, and the odor once again attacked my senses. Shut up was sounding like a better option all the time. I looked back and saw five teenage guys watching me wavering at the door. No backing down now, or I would never hear the end of it. I plunged in, determined to conquer or be conquered.

I slid open the shower door and peered in. It was worse than I had imagined. A brown, encrusted goo hung on the sides of the shower. I aimed my spray bottle of strong chemicals in and began pumping furiously, thoroughly saturating the sides and bottom, and then quickly retreated to the fresh air outside.

Back inside I attacked with the scrub brush and the goo started peeling off in layers. Layer after layer came off as the strong cleaning agents worked overtime. As each layer glopped to the bottom of the tub, I scooped it up and plopped it in a heavy-duty garbage bag. Then it was spray and repeat. The toxic combination of cleaning supplies and incumbent smells necessitated taking frequent breaks to gasp in some fresh air.

Three hours and eight layers later, it was beginning to look better. My runaway student abruptly reappeared at the bathroom door.

"Umm..." he began. "I've been thinking about things, Pastor Don. And I've been feeling a little guilty for running off. So, if you really ...," long pause, "... um ... want me to ...," big swallow, "... work on that shower ...," extremely long pause while choosing his words carefully, "... I guess I will ...," adding rapidly, "... so you can get started on that toilet."

I had almost forgotten. He handed me a new toilet seat, and I relinquished the scrub brushes and chemicals. Still wearing my heavy gloves, I tried to lift the seat. It was stuck fast. There was a black and brown substance holding it tight. I went out to the trailer, procured a long, thick screwdriver, a wrench, and a Makita cordless drill, and set out to find the screws that kept the lid attached. Using the long screwdriver, I pried the seat loose and as it popped up, suddenly a whole new smell emerged. The kid and I both ran, gagging and retching, outdoors. It was then I spotted what was to be our new friend. On top of an army stretcher piled high with junk, that some of the boys were carrying out to the barn, lay a rather large box fan.

"Wait!" I shouted. "Does that thing still work?"

"Dunno," came the response, "didn't try it."

My bathroom buddy and I were on it like flies on stink. We hauled it to the nearest outlet and plugged it in. Miraculously the blades started spinning, and we felt like we had won a small victory.

We hauled it into the bathroom and put it in the already open window. We plugged it in and immediately the stench eased. Just as quickly, however, the people hauling stuff past the window started yelling and gagging as the toxic air spewed forth.

It was back to work. I chipped and scraped the offending substances into the toilet and flushed, repeating the process until I was down to the porcelain. A few borrowed chemicals and scrub brushes soon had it looking good. Now to the seat.

Scraping down, I located the screws and carved out a slot on top. Then kneeling down, I realized that there was no dignified way to change a toilet seat. You simply cannot accomplish the task without hugging the bowl. Working furiously, again with "air breaks," I worked on breaking the nuts loose. The first took about forty-five minutes; the second about twenty-five. (I learned some tricks on the first one that helped with the second.) Needless to say, it was one of the most nauseating, disgusting tasks I've ever undertaken.

As I knelt there hugging that bowl, suddenly the thought struck me: *Is this what it means to be a servant of Jesus Christ?* And as I reflected on the life of Jesus, coming from all of heaven's glory and splendor down to the dump Satan has made of His creation, the toilet bowl of the universe, if you will, with the ugly mold and goo of sin growing from our hearts, I had to concede that I was probably closer to being a disciple, hugging Ed's "tohlet," than I had ever been. For we are never more like Jesus than when we serve.

Jesus called them together and said, "You know that those who are regarded as rulers of the Gentiles lord it over them, and their high officials exercise authority over them. Not so with you. Instead, whoever wants to become great among you must be your servant, and whoever wants to be first must be slave of all. For even the Son of Man did not come to be served, but to serve, and to give his life as a ransom for many. (Mark 10:42–45)

CHAPTER 6
COPS

The mall had just closed, and I had barely left the mall parking lot, heading down a street lined with condos, when suddenly I found myself in a scene reminiscent of a special episode of COPS. A police car just ahead of me had pulled in behind a white Suzuki wagon, and a second police car had stopped just behind the first, but partly blocking my lane. A blue Chevy pickup facing the same direction sat angled across the left side of the road with enough room between it and the police car for my car to ease through. Thinking it was a minor fender bender, I started to ease between the two cars when a man in a brown leather jacket brandishing a drawn revolver leaped from in front of the truck and banged on my hood.

"Stop!!" he cried. "Back up ... NOW!"

No argument here. I slammed the car into reverse and started to back up when two more cruisers, lights flashing, pulled beside and behind me. Another cruiser came screaming down the road in front of me and parked in between the blue pickup and the other police car. I was trapped. For the next twenty minutes, I sat there trying to stare past the flashing lights and watch the unfolding drama in the beam of the strong searchlight mounted on the first patrol car.

"Driver, get out of the car with your hands on your head!" A voice sounded from the grill of the patrol car. Around the scene, about nine officers, both male and female, stood with guns drawn, aimed at the car. A tall, large-boned, heavyset teen struggled to get out of the tiny car without using his hands that he had placed on his head.

"Everyone else put your hands on the inside ceiling of the vehicle." Through the spinning whirl of lights, I could see other hands being slowly raised to the roof.

I looked back to the driver who was now standing with his hands behind his head. He looked to be a young man of about eighteen or nineteen years of age. He was imposing in stature, and the whirling lights revealed a face that did not seem overly concerned with his current predicament.

The commands through the loudspeaker continued. "Kneel down—keep your hands on your head." He struggled to kneel in his baggy denim shorts, while keeping his hands on his head.

"He's still too close," shouted one of the other officers.

Again the voice through the loudspeaker, "Stand up!" He struggled again, trying to keep his hands on his head as he rose to his feet. "Walk backwards." He complied. "Kneel down." Once back down on his knees, five officers rushed in and quickly handcuffed him. They pulled him to his feet and steered him to one of the waiting patrol cars right next to where I was trapped. Placing a hand on top of his head to keep him from bumping it, one of the officers guided his descent into the back seat. Still, he did not seem overly concerned. A cool, arrogance seemed to pervade his gaze as he looked over at me. I turned my attention back to the ongoing drama.

"Passenger in the front seat," called the loudspeaker voice, "come out slowly with your hands up."

The passenger from the front seat was a girl who looked to be about sixteen or seventeen. She was tall, slender, and very attractive with long, dark hair. She had no look of arrogance or cool. She was visibly shaken by the experience she now found herself in the middle of. Tears streamed down her face as she cried out, "Don't shoot me, please."

"Back up and kneel down," said the voice. She did and two officers quickly had her handcuffed and led her to another waiting car. She sobbed uncontrollably as she passed between my car and the one where the driver sat watching coolly. She saw him in the back of the car next to mine and screamed at him through her tears. He just stared straight ahead, unwilling to meet her gaze. She was deposited in the car behind mine.

"Passenger in the back seat, come out slowly with your hands on your head."

The heavyset girl in the back seat bent down as if to pick something up. Nine officers with guns all aimed at her started screaming, "Get your hands up where we can see them." She looked back over her shoulder into the glaring spotlight. A look of defiance clearly marked her features.

"Come out of the car with your hands on your head!" the voice repeated more sternly.

"Come and get me," she mouthed into the light at no one in particular.

The loudspeaker voice intoned, "You have ten seconds to come out of the car or we will come in. These officers have been authorized to shoot."

> **"You have ten seconds to come out of the car or we will come in. These officers have been authorized to shoot."**

Was I going to watch someone get shot right in front of me? "Please, girl, come out with your hands up," I pleaded silently.

Suddenly the back door burst open, and the girl started to make a break. The guy in the car next to me laughed and cheered her on. Instantly there were five cops on her. She struggled and kicked and even tried to bite one of the officers, but they soon had her subdued in handcuffs. As they pulled her to her feet, a defiant sneer crossed her face.

When they led her past my headlights, to put her in the

car to my left, she was almost laughing at them. She saw me watching her from my car, and she shot me a look of searing scorn. I held her gaze but inwardly flinched. I had seen that look before.

Defiance, hatred, and a determination were there. How does one get to this state? It is in the daily decisions; the decisions that come to each of us from moment to moment. It is in the decisions to serve self rather than God. With each decision, we begin to look more like whichever side we choose. And the more choices toward Satan, the more the look begins to be fixed.

It is the look of one who has beheld and idolized the dark side one day at a time until, little by little, they become so controlled by the enemy of our souls that they fail to realize the extent of his control. It is the look of one who, thinking they are being their own person and making their own decisions, are unable to recognize how deeply they have moved into Satan's territory. Even as the noose tightens around their neck, they continue to insist that they are free and nothing can touch them; they are above the law. It is the look of one who has taken on the appearance of a greater master.

It was apparent that, though she was young, Satan had left his mark on this one. I could almost see him laughing through her. She jerked her head away from the guiding hand of the officer and banged her head on the top of the door. "Don't touch my #@$*# head," she screamed as she fell backward into the car.

Once they put her in the car, they moved the pickup truck aside and let me go through.

As I drove on home, I couldn't help thinking about that look. It haunted me. And then I began thinking about me. And my church. What are we doing to help ones with "the look"? What responsibility do we have for those going to hell? Not just those who come to our youth groups, but ones that inhabit our neighborhoods. What is our responsibility to our community?

Have we taken our call to "come out of her, My people" so seriously, that we refuse to engage any but those who show up to our evangelism series or send in a Bible study card? Are we unwilling to take Jesus back into the world?

Has it ever occurred to any of us that Jesus called us to love even those with "the look"? To pursue them in love and let them know that they aren't stuck with that sneer, that hatred and scorn.

Jesus said, "By this everyone will know that you are my disciples, if you love one another" (John 13:35). Do they see it in you?

CHAPTER 7

The Nerd Factory

Who makes them? Is there a factory somewhere? How come we seem to have so many of them running around? Where *do* nerds *come from?*

Everywhere you look, there are nerds (or nerdettes) running around. You know the type: They don't know when to be quiet, they drop their tray in the cafeteria, they wear half-matching clothes, and most of them know the cube root of an airplane propeller (or at least could find it with the help of their trusty, ever-present calculator.)

I befriended a real nerd a few years ago, and as soon as it seemed safe, I asked him that question. "Where did you come from?"

His reply was typically nerdy. "From my parents," he said.

Seeing that I wasn't getting anywhere, I began relentlessly interrogating the nerd in search of some clue to answer my question. I asked about his parents, his clothes, and even the cube root of an airplane propeller (he didn't know). Now, in hopes of helping all of us, I will report my findings. I must let you know that I have found, at least in part, the answer to this perplexing question.

Let me tell you his story.

Alan was born young, as many nerds are. But he didn't know that he was destined to be a nerd for life, because actually Alan was very normal at birth. He did things like normal kids do. It wasn't until later that he began developing nerd tendencies.

At first, the problem centered in Alan's parents. They didn't want him. He was, as they told him many times, an "accident." A ruining of their lives. At best, he was a major intrusion into their already-rocky relationship.

And he was hard to take care of in their nomadic existence. They had to be up early to get their trailer into the best slot at the flea market of whatever town they happened to be in. And to stop and feed a baby, or to chase him down as a toddler, was a huge bother. Sometimes too much of a bother. Mostly he had to go hungry or put up with being locked in a tiny trailer closet most of the day so he wouldn't wander off. Sometimes when he cried, he got beat severely. I mean, who was he to get hungry at their busiest time? So what if he was only one-year-old? The kid had to learn patience and obedience.

Alan grew, and as state laws dictate, he had to be put in school. His parents couldn't afford to pay the fines for keeping him out of school. But putting him in school would restrict their travels and their income.

To make matters worse, they had another "accident" about this time and were having to teach this new one the hard facts of life like they had taught Alan. They finally decided to settle in a community close to a large metropolitan area. At least while, Alan was in school, they could lock the younger one in the closet and go sell at the flea market.

Life for Alan was getting more complicated. He tried to do well in school, but he had problems understanding everything. It probably had something to do with the time, at age three, when his dad knocked him unconscious and fractured his skull. But Alan never thought of that. He only knew that he wasn't as quick as the other kids. He'd heard his teacher tell his mom and dad that he was very slow, and that's why he needed to repeat the first grade. On the way home his dad cursed him for being stupid.

It probably had something to do with the time, at age three, when his dad knocked him unconscious and fractured his skull.

Learning wasn't the only area that caused him problems. Some of the other kids said he smelled funny. Some said that he had a bowl haircut (before it was popular). Others simply laughed and pushed him away whenever he asked to play with them. Sometimes he didn't mind, but sometimes it made him mad, and soon he was labeled a discipline problem for fighting with the other kids. His dad beat him severely for being so violent with other kids.

By the time Alan reached the third grade, the other kids absolutely despised him, and his teacher simply tolerated him. The other parents talked about him, the principal knew him well, and the cafeteria director was totally disgusted with the way he "snarfed down" his food at lunch. "Why, it's as if he hadn't eaten in a week!" she exclaimed.

One day Alan's dad dropped him off at school (it was kind of embarrassing to climb out of their beat-up motor home) and told him he would pick him up at 3:00 p.m. as usual. Alan said good-bye and went on into his third-grade room. At 3:00 p.m. he wandered outside and waited for the old "rolling garbage can," as some of his classmates called the motor home. But it never showed up.

He waited: 4:00 p.m., 5:00 p.m., 6:00 p.m., 7:30 p.m. And he was really getting hungry.

The police caught him digging through the trash dumpster behind a local college cafeteria. They took him to the trailer park where he lived and dropped him off.

His parent's motor home wasn't there, so Alan went to the office. "They checked out about 10:00 this morning. Paid their bill up and pulled out. Didn't say where they were going. They musta left you behind accidental-like."

Alan crawled underneath another trailer and curled up to sleep. He would look for them in the morning.

Three days and sixty-five miles later, he found them at a flea market in a neighboring town.

"How did you find us, you little jerk? You were supposed to find somewhere else to go. Don't you know by now that we don't want you?" His dad drove him back to school and drove away.

The pattern that had begun three days prior was repeated again and again until Alan's parents finally gave up.

At school, it didn't go without notice that whenever Alan did come, his clothes were dirty, his hair was uncombed, his face and hands were filthy, and he took unusually large portions in the cafeteria at lunch. Alan learned that society is cruel and vicious to people who don't look just right. The more his classmates teased and taunted him, the more Alan lashed out at them. Yet he wanted their acceptance more than anything.

By eighth grade, Alan was considered a real nerd. He tried to fit in, but his vile mouth and nerdlike ways won him more rejection, more lunch hours by himself, and no friends. If anyone did feel sorry for him and show him the least bit of attention, Alan would dog the person's steps like a puppy gone mad with affection. Of course, this would inevitably end in rejection because he would drive the person right up the wall.

Upon Alan's graduation, his dad heard about a school that boarded kids—an academy, they called it. And his dad found out that a kid could work off most of his bill. So he dropped Alan off at the academy in midsummer. That's where I met him.

Alan was always grinning stupidly or fighting, either loudmouthed or foulmouthed, always dressed wrong, and always so insanely dumb that he could be nothing but a real-life nerd.

Alan was always grinning stupidly or fighting, either loudmouthed or foulmouthed, always dressed wrong, and always so insanely dumb that he could be nothing but a real-life nerd. *A case study in the making,* I thought. At least, that's what I thought until our conversation.

As we talked, I suddenly began to realize that Alan was the way he was because of the people around him: his parents, his elementary classmates, and people like me, who are so incredibly blind and insensitive that we heap more rejection on someone who needs so badly the acceptance we could offer. I mean, what would you or I be like if we'd been treated like Alan all of our lives?

My conclusion? There really is a "nerd factory." And its workers are those of us who constantly dole out large or small doses of rejection. Those of us who make fun of or play jokes on the nerds in our life. When we try to make ourselves look better by climbing high on the broken pieces of those we destroy daily, we are worse off than any nerd.

Is it possible that Jesus could have been referring in part to nerds as "the least of these brothers and sisters of mine" (Matt. 25:40)? Or might Paul have had nerds in mind when he wrote, "Do not think of yourself more highly than you ought," but "in humility value others above yourselves" (Rom. 12:3; Phil. 2:3)?

I don't know about you, but I've decided to quit the "nerd factory" and begin working at the "De-Nerding Center for Socially Deprived Children of God." It's going to be a hard and dirty job, but the way I see it, someone's got to do it. And from what I hear, they have lots of positions available. Need an application?

CHAPTER 8

Roadmaps, Rappelling, and the Big, Dark Woods

With acknowledgment to Dick Duerksen for his creative book-mark series that sparked the idea for, and forms the basis of, this chapter.

I thought it would be fun to take this entire chapter and go through all twenty-eight of the Adventist's fundamental beliefs. OK. Actually, I'd like to give you five short stories that may help explain them a little better.

Story #1 – Roadmaps and Rulebooks

I went to college in the late 70s at what was then known as Southern Missionary College in Collegedale, Tennessee. There's nothing unusual about that. My parents lived in Arizona. Here's where the problem lay. If you know anything about United States geography, you know that there was no quick route home. As a matter of fact, during the days of the fifty-five-mile-per-hour speed limit, it took about thirty hours by car to go between the two. That's a long way to drive by oneself. So I didn't.

My cousin Paul, who also attended Southern, but lived

six hours further away in Southern California, purchased the coolest truck from the California Highway Department road crew. It was a 1972 Dodge step-side pickup. Oh, it didn't look like much when he bought it. Road-crew yellow. Plain. Ugly. Not the sort of vehicle college guys try attracting women with. The only ones that would have been attracted to it would be ones that naturally wear safety vests around the house—which weren't exactly the types that we were interested in. We, at least, wanted ones with a full set of teeth.

Anyway, back to the truck. After he and his dad did a makeover, this thing was one cool ride! Metallic-blue paint job. Mag wheels. A topper on the back with a fully carpeted deck to stretch out a sleeping bag or two and plenty of room underneath to pack all of our luggage. Along with all of that, in keeping with the rage of the late 70s, it had a nice Cobra CB radio to communicate with all the truckers across the country. And for internal communication, there were windows in between the cab and the back for shouting through or even crawling between when we were tired of one or the other.

Once my cousin had completed the makeover, and knowing that my '69 Ambassador Rambler was on its last leg, he called to offer to share the truck with me at college if I would help him drive it across each time. I was game. Three days later he pulled into my driveway driving what he had now dubbed "The Blue Burrito," ready to head east. What a setup! One could stretch out in the back and one could drive. We could drive it straight through and feel good when we got there. It turned out to be a great way to go.

By Christmas there were many more "westerners" wanting to ride with us. We quickly calculated that with six of us in the truck at fourteen miles per gallon, if we split the gas cost among everyone, we could get by on about $20 each cross-country. (This is back when gas was at an unbelievable high of $.88 per gallon. Hard to fathom, I know. We were outraged.)

We crammed four in the back in sleeping bags and put two in the cab. Since there was no heat in the back, we figured that four across would add extra warmth, with the warmest sleeping bags on the outsides. In the cab, one would, of course, be the driver, while the other rode "shotgun." The person riding "shotgun" would be responsible for navigating through the cities to make sure we stayed on Interstate 40 and didn't end up heading north or south. We would rotate teams every two hours for safety and to let someone in the back sit up for a while as well as warm up, and let the driver and navigator lay down in the back for some shut-eye. In this manner, we figured that we would always have an alert driver and navigator. Besides, after four hours in the back, you were ready to get out and do anything but lay down.

We divided into three teams of two. Since each person would only drive every other time their team came around, we figured that each person would only have to drive nine of the thirty hours to Phoenix. Paul would have to drive the additional six hours to Southern California himself.

It was 4:00 a.m. The back of the topper door was abruptly jerked open and cold air blasted in, and awoke us. "Keele, Jansen—your turn to drive." Paul was already scrambling for his shoes, knowing that he was the next driver, and as such, he had to pump the gas so that he would be fully awake to drive. I slid out of the back and just slipped my feet far enough into my shoes to allow me to step on the heels and tiptoe around to the cab. I was seat-belted into the "shotgun" position in the warm cab in no time, and with my head on a pillow against the door, was quickly back in dreamland.

Abruptly Paul jerked open the door, slid in behind the wheel, and slammed the door. I sat up, eyes half-open. "Well, navigator," Paul said, "Which way?"

"Wha?" I half responded.

"Which way?"

"West, you dufus!" I leaned my head back against the door and started back to slumber city.

"Yeah, that's what I mean? Where's the freeway, and which way is west?"

I sat up and looked around. The station that the last team had selected was out in the middle of nowhere. Looking all around us, I couldn't see the freeway either north or south of us.

"So do we go left or right?" Paul asked.

"Go left ... no right ... no—hold on." I opened the little window from the cab to the back, but they had the topper window shut tight against the cold. I banged. No one moved.

I got out and walked around and jerked open the back window. "Hey, which way is the freeway?" I shouted. One guy looked up and said, "It's down there," and pointed toward the roof of the topper. He abruptly broke into a snore, and I was sure there would be no more helpful information coming from his direction. The other three never moved.

I closed the topper door and walked back around to the cab.

"Do you think we should ask for directions back in the station?" Paul queried.

"What, and break the man-code?" I gave him a shocked look. "No—we'll find it! Besides, I got a small clue from the deadheads in the back. They said, it was 'down there', so that means we need to turn South. So go left." I was proud of my powers of deduction, and Paul seemed to be satisfied.

He turned the "Blue Burrito" left and we headed out. After about three miles, he turned to me and asked, "Are you sure this is the right way."

"Well, no, not exactly."

"Why don't you check the map?"

I flipped on the cigarette lighter, flexible-necked map light from Kmart and opened the glove compartment and started fishing around.

"Will you look at this?" I exclaimed, drawing out a California Highway driver's manual. I flipped it open and began to read.

"Seat belts are now required of all occupants traveling in a motor vehicle. You got your seat belt on?"

> "Do you think we should ask for directions back in the station?" Paul queried.
>
> "What, and break the man-code?" I gave him a shocked look. "No—we'll find it!

"Yes, but are we going the right way?" Paul countered.

"If you've got your seat belt on and I've got mine on—looks like we're doing fine. Oh, look at this. It says you are not supposed to follow any emergency vehicle closer than 500 feet." I scanned the dark horizon. "Look, dude, I can't even see any emergency vehicles, so we're doing great!"

"Yeah," Paul said weakly, "but are we going the right way?"

Point #1 – The Bible is the Word of God—not a rulebook, but a roadmap.

Hebrews 4:12 says, "For the word of God is alive and active. Sharper than any double-edged sword, it penetrates even to dividing soul and spirit, joints and marrow; it judges the thoughts and attitudes of the heart."

Second Peter 1:21 says, "For prophecy never had its origin in the human will, but prophets, though human, spoke from God as they were carried along by the Holy Spirit."

The Bible isn't there to just let you know all of the rules. God gave you the Bible to help you get where you need to go—heaven. Has it ever occurred to you that you could be doing everything right and still miss The Way?

> *NOTE: For those of you who remain curious. Yes, we did turn around, and yes, we found the freeway about four miles back.*

Story #2—Grandma's House.

My grandma's house hasn't changed in fifty years. Well, OK, there was the addition of vinyl siding and central heat and air, but besides that, it still looks the same. My grandfather built the house back in the 1950s when they moved to Collegedale, Tennessee, for my dad to go to college. But ever since I was born, I've only known that house as "Grandma's house." To be sure, Granddaddy lived there too, and sometimes we'd say that we were headed to "Grandma and Granddaddy's" house. But to keep things short and simple, it was "Grandma's house."

I *loved* to go to Grandma's house. It had the best brick wall on the side of the carport that went halfway up to the roofline, and from there, two sets of fan-shaped poles bolted to the top of the wall held the roof up.

Early on, my cousins and I would have to stretch to reach the bottom of the poles on the top of the wall, and we would strain to pull ourselves up, while our bare feet wind-milled their way up the red brick. Once on top of the wall, we could go back and forth along it for what seemed to be hours without getting bored. We would swing around the poles and balance along the wall until all of a sudden, something more exciting would capture the attention of one of us on the wall, and off they would go. Once one person had jumped down to run off, the others were sure to follow if the new pursuit was indeed more exciting than the wall.

There were lots of exciting things to do at grandma's house. The tree swing. The tree house. Running through the sprinkler on a hot day. Games of Simon Says and Mother, May I and of course, the favorite on the large front lawn was Red Light, Green Light.

We also each had to take our turn helping granddaddy plant the garden, water the garden, fertilize the garden, weed the garden, or pick the garden as well. "The garden" was actually two and a half acres of plowed ground on either side of the house from which corn, popcorn, watermelons, cantaloupes, okra, squashes of all kinds, beans of more kinds, peppers, radishes, lettuce, and all sorts of other great things grew. We knew it was hard work because we all had to help and our small hands and backs would grow very tired until finally we were released from the hard labor. Then we would head back up to the house, and with our last ounce of strength, pull ourselves back up to the top of the wall, where we would sit and brag about who did the most work in the garden.

But my favorite thing of all at Grandma's house is what happened when I first got there. As a kid, I was usually one of the first out of the car and into the house, so I could hear it. The greeting. It usually went something like this.

"Hey, kid, c'mon in. Sit down and rest your feet. Can I get you something to eat?" (I loved that last part!) If Grandma was busy she'd just say, "Look in the refrigerator and see what you want. I'm just saving ..." and she would list what we couldn't touch in the fridge. Everything else was fair game.

> **"Hey, kid, c'mon in. Sit down and rest your feet. Can I get you something to eat?"**

I still loved going to Grandma's house even as an adult. It wasn't because of the wall, though my kids enjoyed it growing up. It wasn't the tree swing or the tree house because they are both long gone. I no longer got jazzed about running through the sprinkler on a hot summer day. Simon Says and Red Light, Green Light are never played there anymore. Even the garden is gone, and in fact, both grandma and granddaddy have passed to their rest.

No. I loved going to Grandma's house because of grandma. And the greeting. No matter how old I got she still called me kid. I walked in a few months before she died and there it was. "Hey, kid, c'mon in. Sit down and rest your feet. There's some cake on the counter if you want something."

Through the good times and the bad of my life, no matter how much life changed around me, I always knew that I could go back to Grandma's house and my acceptance there was always automatic and unconditional. That never changed.

Grandma passed away a few years ago and we had to sell the old place. It has changed forever. I miss her for many reasons, but I especially miss her love and acceptance, because there are so few things in this life that you can always count on. As a matter of fact, I've only discovered one.

Point #2 – Jesus Christ is the One who never changes in a universe that always does.

The Bible says, "Jesus Christ is the same yesterday and today and forever" (Heb. 13:8).

Paul wrote, "And he was shown to be the Son of God when he was raised from the dead by the power of the Holy Spirit.

He is Jesus Christ our Lord" (Rom. 1:4, NLT).

And God said, "This is my Son, whom I love. Listen to him!" (Mark 9:7).

Wouldn't it be nice to know that you have a place to go that never changes? A place where you know you are safe and loved. May I suggest Jesus? He never changes. Your acceptance with Him is always automatic and unconditional. That will never change.

Story #3 – Family Photo Albums

My mother loves photo albums. Oh, it's not just the albums. She loves taking the pictures for them. Growing up I can't remember an event where she didn't have a camera in her hands. For years it was the Kodak Instamatic with the little flash-cubes that rotated on the top after each picture. She used to buy those flash-cubes in bulk. It's obvious by our photo albums that my sisters got preferential treatment.

See, for each of us kids, Mom started a photo album. All the pictures she took of each of us went into our individual photo album. One for Pam, my eldest sister, then me, then Rusty, my kid brother, and then years later, Michelle, my baby sister. Each photo album chronicled each life. All of the birthdays, vacations, big events, and candids went in. Then there were the school pictures.

I hated those things. You know the ones. Your teacher lets you go to the bathroom to check your hair in a mirror. Then you head back to the classroom where you fill out the information card. Once your card is filled out, you get in a line. Next, you walk into the school gymnasium or cafeteria or library or wherever the photographer happened to set up for that year. Then they process you.

"Hand me your card please," the photographer's assistant would chirp. Then she would make some sort of comment about each one. "Oh, you're a cutie." "How precious." "Look at this gorgeous doll." "You must be an angel from heaven." When my turn came, she said, "My, that's a colorful shirt." Then you go to "the stool of unnatural positions."

The photographer would say, "next please" in a voice that was neither friendly nor unfriendly—just kind of bored and flat-toned. He would then grab the stool and deftly raise or lower it to accommodate your particular body size. Next he would position you on the stool and walk around behind his camera. After making adjustments to the height of the camera and very quickly checking his lighting, he would try to get your body into a position that would rival the moves of the world's best contortionist.

"OK, we'll put your knees pointing this direction. Lean forward. Turn your head slightly to the left. Good. Chin down. Tilt the top of your head slightly to the right. Chin down. Good. Look into the camera." Then he would say the line that almost always cracked me up. "Look natural and SMILE."

And I always wanted to say, "Buddy, I don't naturally put myself into this body position, so there's no way I can look natural while I'm here. Smile, maybe—but it sure won't look natural."

Of course, I never said anything, because it would have broken both my pose and his thinly veiled veneer of patience, so I just tried to smile and look as natural as one can in that uncomfortable position. Click. Flash. And your torture was over.

"Next please." And you got to watch your buddy behind you squirm on the stool as his body was forced to do unnatural things. They would hand you an information card to take home to your parents, and barring any horrible mishaps requiring retakes, you could rest easy for another year—or at least until the pictures came.

Most years they would hand them out at school and the comparison games would begin. "Let me see yours! Ha! You look like a dork!"

"Oh yeah? Well, let me see yours? Well you look like a contortionist!"

"Well, that's not *my* fault! That photographer made me get in that position."

You would dutifully take them home, and your parents would decide whether they wanted them or not and send the money back in the supplied envelope. Naturally, my mother always bought them, and naturally they went into my book, which was rapidly becoming the world's guide to human contortions.

That system changed my seventh-grade year. Actually, we moved to another state, I changed schools, and the new school was trying out a new system. Instead of the teachers having to go through the hassle of trying to get everyone's money or their pictures back, it was announced that this year everything would be pre-paid, and the photographer would mail them in a special cellophane-panel envelope directly to your home. No money. No pictures. If you didn't like your pictures for any reason, there would be guaranteed retakes until you were happy.

I decided I would be happy with the first time around, since retakes would bring on the "humorous" remarks from your classmates. Oh, I had heard the comments from the class clowns to those who had to get retakes when their name was called. "What, you broke the camera the first time so they had to come back with a special beefed-up 'no-break' camera just for you?" Hahahahaha. Or: "It doesn't matter how many times they do it, they can't fix it, because they got nothin' to work with!" Hahahaha. Or: "Hey, keep your mouth shut this time so the flash doesn't bounce off your braces and blind the photographer." Hahahaha.

Not only had I heard the class clowns spewing forth such comments, I had joined in. OK. Sometimes I started it, thinking I was being clever. So why would anyone who made those comments want to go back for retakes until they were happy? Be happy the first time, because it probably wouldn't get much better anyway.

Let me digress just enough to tell you that I was not much of a looker in the seventh-grade. As a matter of fact, I didn't lose my two front teeth until the third grade, and I had already started playing trumpet by then, so in the absence of my two front teeth, my gums became rock hard as I practiced my trumpet. Unbeknownst to me, it didn't stop my two front teeth from growing, it just didn't allow them to cut through the now-thick gums. I went almost ten months without front teeth, all the while they were growing up toward my brain. When I began having severe headaches, we went to the dentist and X-rays revealed my need for help in freeing my front incisors. A few pain injections and a sharp dental tool cutting through my numb gums quickly set them free. My teeth dropped down half an inch in the first hour, and to my horror, I discovered that, not only did I have two front teeth instantly, but they were HUGE! They were way bigger than the rest of the teeth I had in my mouth, and I instantly earned a nickname from my loving, elder sister.

"Beaver, beaver ... you are a beaver," she exclaimed as she saw them for the first time. "You know," she continued, "I read that if beavers don't gnaw on something, their teeth will grow into their brain and they will die. Do you want something to chew on?"

School the next day was no better. In fact, it was worse. My teeth became a hot boredom-busting topic. You got nothing else to talk about? How about MY TEETH?

Fast-forward back to the seventh grade. The only thing that had changed was that I had lost all of my baby teeth, so my other teeth were now a bit larger, but still no match for my "killer fangs," as one of my new classmates had dubbed them. Only he had such great wit as to warp my last name into the mix as well when he called them "Keele-r Fangs," trying to put a fake Hispanic accent on my name to make it sound like he was saying "killer fangs." As in, "You got some real Keele-r Fangs, Senor!" Bahahahahaha.

"Did your mother have any kids that lived?" I retorted.

To which he only gave me a confused look and said, "What do you mean?"

"Never mind," I replied, "it's obvious she didn't." He was unfazed.

"Do you have any venom in those Keele-r Fangs?" Bahahahaha. "Don't bite me, if you do, Senor!" Bahahahaha.

Back to the story. Picture day in seventh grade. New photographer. New protocol. Pay in advance. Retakes until you're happy. Yeah, right.

"Next please." Some things never change. There was the stool of torture. He deftly adjusted it for my body. He quickly positioned me on the stool and then walked around behind his camera. After making adjustments to the height of his camera and very quickly checking his lighting, it was contortionist time. Only this guy was like a hyperactive squirrel on caffeine. Everything came in rapid-fire, machine gun cadence.

"OK. We'll put your knees pointing this direction. Lean forward. Turn your head slightly to the left. Good. Chin down. Tilt the top of your head slightly to the right. Chin down. Good. Look into the camera. Look natural and SMILE. WAIT!"

What? Wait? Wait for what?

"Your lips look a little dry, son. Why don't you lick your lips?" he said as his trigger finger toyed with the button on his wired remote. "Go ahead, quickly now," he continued. "We have lots of other children to photograph."

I was halfway through licking my lips ... that is, I had wet my top lip and big teeth with my tongue and was using the back of my big teeth to wet my bottom lip, when his twitching trigger finger got the better of him. Click. Flash. "Next please."

"Um, wait. Could we do that over? I was like this," I said as I put my protruding incisors out in front of my lower lip.

"We'll do it over on retake day if you aren't happy with it. Next please," he said all in one breath.

"No, you don't understand," I pleaded. "That picture will make me look like a beaver or killer fangs or something that I don't want to look like. Can't you just take another one now?"

"On retake day ... not a moment sooner. Move along. Next please."

The laughter of my classmates faded into the distance as my world closed in around me. All I could think about was a special cellophane-paneled envelope showing up in our mailbox. All of the postal workers would have a good laugh. I could hear them now. Probably even with New York mobster accents.

"Hey Chah-lie! Get a load of 'dis kid! Looks like a beav-ah or somethun."

"Is 'dat right? Lemme see ... whoa ... poor kid. Looks like he needs to gnaw on somethun. Ya know, I read somewhere dat if beavers don't gnaw on somethun 'deir teeth will grow right up into 'deir brain and kill 'em."

> **I could hear them now. Probably even with New York mobster accents. "Hey Chah-lie! Get a load of 'dis kid! Looks like a beav-ah or somethun."**

"No kiddin'? Wow, maybe we should have Mavis put a note on 'dis one when she delivers it to warn his mo-thuh. She could at leas' stock some celery or somethun'."

I shook my head and cleared the images out of my imagination. Then a thought more horrifying hit me. What if Pam found them first? I'd never hear the end of it. I determined to be the first one to the mailbox every day until they came.

Two weeks later I opened the mailbox to see three cellophane-paneled envelopes staring back at me. The top one was my brother. Third-grade. Lively. Energetic. And the photographer's assistant always said, "Oh, aren't you a cutie!"

Next, was my sister's. Eighth grade. Long-hair. Sophisticated, and secretly, though I would never admit it out loud to her, I thought she was beautiful.

On the bottom, probably out of pity for "that poor beaver-kid," lay mine. It was as bad as I had expected. Two giant pearly whites shining forth like beacons in the night. I rapidly developed a plan. I took the mail inside and removed my envelope from the pile.

Quickly running downstairs, I lifted up my mattress and slid them under. No need to open the envelope and stare at thirty-six more identical pictures. If you don't like the 8x10, you definitely won't like the 5x7's, the 3x5's, and the twenty wallets "for trading with your friends."

Instantly, to avoid my siblings, I set about doing my chores. I said nothing about the mail, and they didn't seem to think of it, so it lay in a pile on the kitchen counter until Mom and Dad came home with my younger sister.

"Oh, look," Mom exclaimed. "Your pictures came! At least Pam and Rusty's are here."

Pam ran to grab her package from Mom's hands while proceeding to do what every eighth-grade female does when they get their pictures, but before they actually see them. "Oh, Mother, those are horrid. Don't let anyone see."

"No, they're not, dear. It's a beautiful likeness of you. Don't you think so, hon?" she asked, showing them to Dad.

"Oh, yes," Dad said, pulling the picture from inside the cellophane envelope and studying it. "You've become a very lovely young lady."

Pam snatched them away from Dad and then proceeded to do what every eighth-grade female does *after* they see their pictures. "Oh, look at these … they're horrid. Look. No. Don't look. What do you think? I think they're simply awful. Look. No. Don't look. Aren't they terrible?" Inwardly you knew she liked them, but she wouldn't be caught dead admitting it.

"Yeah, you're right," Rusty said looking over her shoulder. "You do look like a real dork."

"You hush your mouth! I wasn't asking you anyway."

Mom was working on opening Rusty's package. "Oh, these are precious! You're so cute! I know that Grandma will like these!"

"Where are yours, Donnie?" my dad suddenly asked.

"Oh, they must not have come yet." I lied, trying to sound convincing.

My younger brother was quick to rat me out. "Um, no. They came. Um. 'Cause I, um, saw him putting them under his mattress in his room."

"You little ratfink!" I started, but was cut short by my dad.

"Go get them, son," he commanded.

"Ah, well, they're really not very good," I began.

"That's what your sister said," my mom responded, "and hers are absolutely beautiful. Now go get yours."

"Well, see," I was grasping for anything to save myself,

but nothing seemed to be forthcoming. Then out of nowhere, "Um ... I think I will need to have retakes, cause I wasn't ready when he took it and the picture came out looking really dumb."

"Well, considering what they had to work with—" my sister started.

Dad cut off the rest of her remark as well as my quickly formulating comeback. "Well, you let us be the judge of that. Go get your pictures—NOW!"

"Yes, sir." I knew it was best not to try and argue the point. I went downstairs to my room and got them. I would have to try a new tactic.

"You have to promise not to laugh," I started as I came back upstairs clutching the cellophane window to my chest.

"We would never laugh at you," my mom countered. "You're our son, and we love you very much. A little picture won't change that."

"Maybe not, but I know you're gonna laugh, and I don't want you to laugh." I shot back. "Promise me you won't laugh."

"OK," said Mom. "We promise not to laugh. Now give them here."

I handed her the cellophane-paneled envelope upside down. She turned it over and with one look at the picture, her hand went over her mouth to stifle a laugh.

"It's cute," she chortled. "I think we should keep it. I'll put it in your album."

"NO! Don't EVER put it in my album!" I shouted.

"Calm down, son," my dad said. Then to my mom, "Let me see it."

He took one look and a big grin came across his face followed by a suppressed chuckle. Next it was my sister's turn. "Beaver, beaver ... you are a beaver!" Then she imitated what she thought a beaver would sound like by rapidly smacking her lips. *Chupchupchupchupchup.*

I was getting angry now. "I told you it was an awful picture, and you promised not to laugh—and now you've broken your promise," I shouted.

"We're not laughing at you," my sister began. "We're laughing with you!"

"Yeah, only I'm not laughing," I shot back angrily. "So that means you're laughing at me, and I don't like it at all."

Fortunately, Mom did concede not to send my school picture to all the relatives that year. But no matter how I pleaded, it still went into the album. And every time I would steal the picture from the album, another would mysteriously appear to take its place. And, why not? She had paid for the whole package.

I'm grown now, with young adult children of my own. We still get together for holidays and birthdays, and sometimes when we are together, out come the old albums. I always know whenever someone is looking at my album, and they turn to the page containing my seventh-grade picture. It still brings a laugh and a comment. And I've learned to laugh at it as well. I did kind of look like a beaver.

Dad died years ago, and Mom lives alone now. Sometimes, she tells me, on a Friday night, she'll pull out all of the albums and go through them. She'll relive the good times and recall stories of our growing-up years. She'll remember how we were at every stage, and yes, she still laughs at that stupid seventh-grade picture. But most of all, she looks forward to the day when we will all be reunited as a family— her, Dad, all of us kids, and now, grandkids. Actually, she doesn't just look forward to that day, she longs for it. But as much as she longs for it, God the Father longs for it more.

Point #3 – God keeps a family album, and my picture is in it.
It's true! God keeps a family album, and my picture is in it. And so is yours. As a matter of fact, He has a family album for each one of us, and He longs for the day when we'll all be home, together for eternity.

But aside from eternity, the Bible says that God loves me and has a plan for my life right now. And He has a plan for your life as well. And He wants to complete His purpose in us so that He can take us home and be reunited with Him for all eternity.

"The Lord will work out his plans for my life—for your faithful love, O Lord, endures forever. Don't abandon me, for you made me" (Ps. 138:8, NLT).

"I have been crucified with Christ and I no longer live, but Christ lives in me. The life I now live in the body, I live by faith in the Son of God, who loved me and gave himself for me" (Gal. 2:20).

Though God longs for the day He can take you and me home; He also longs for the day that you and I will learn to live our lives according to His purpose and through His strength. As He turns the pages of His family album, He relives those days that we lived with Him and it makes Him long all the more for the day when He will reunite His family for eternity.

Story #4 – Indoor Rappelling.

Somewhere in my younger life, I got the impression that to be a good Christian one had to look like they had just sucked on a lemon and have breath that smelled like they had refused dental care because of the Lord's imminent return, as it would just be a waste of money.

I think I got the impression from a few of the older ladies in our church when I was growing up, one in particular, who backed me into the corner of the church porch with her cane and wilted me down with both her breath, and a verbal barrage about not "being ready for the kingdom with behavior" like mine. Her style of Christianity was fine, I guess, but it sure didn't appeal to me. Besides, I reasoned, if she were going to the kingdom, it would be reason enough for me to stay away.

I just wasn't wired that way. I had a hard time keeping my mind on anything very long. If there was any lull in the action, I could think of something to occupy it. My mind would race along with new ideas popping in all the time. I just never knew when something new would come in. And I wasn't always good at deciding whether it was a good idea or a bad one until I had tried it.

"Wherever did you come up with that idea?" my second-grade substitute asked after she discovered all of the boys in their seats after recess and mud on the windowsill. During recess one of my friends and I had been discussing the "girls are always first" rule. He had stated that he didn't like waiting all of that time, because he felt some of the girls took advantage at the water fountain and drank like camels and used up all of the guys time to get a drink. Then we were all told to cut it short because we needed to get back to class.

I simply observed that it was actually a shorter distance to the ground-level windows of our classroom than back around the building to line up. All of the guys could climb through the windows, I reasoned, have their drinks and be in their seats before the girls line got there. We would tell the substitute that our teacher always let us do that to save her time. What did substitutes know anyway? We passed the word and Operation Windowsill was born.

It worked as planned, except that I hadn't factored in the substitute's lack of patience as she waited with all of the girls in the hot sun outside. I also hadn't figured it would actually get us in trouble since we didn't do any damage. All of us got marched back down the hall and had to line up outside, and then each of us got a whack on the seat with the paddle as we were then sternly told, "Now WALK down the hall and to your desk."

Then there was the time in seventh grade when my friend Charlie and I decided to test the theory of gradually increasing the temperature of water on a frog to see if it would jump out. It didn't. Stupid frog actually stayed in and met his demise.

Or the time in high school when another friend and I put on garbage cans with a "push" lid, and tried to follow the night watchman that we had dubbed "Barney Fife," up the center campus sidewalk. Each time he would spin around with flashlight in hand, we would stoop down on the side of the sidewalk in the garbage cans. "Hmmm," he would mutter, "I could have sworn I heard something." It would have worked if we hadn't gotten fancy and tried to crisscross the sidewalk each time. As we were running across, we accidentally banged into each other. When he spun around this time, he found himself face to face with two garbage cans *with legs!* It was hard outrunning him with those cans, but somehow we managed.

So, given my history of unique ideas coming from a lull in the action, it should have been no surprise that my History of Western Civilization class in college became a veritable think tank. A time of churning out the ideas. Some good. Some not. But who's to know till you try?

History was at 1:00 p.m. And, as any college student can tell you, there is no worse time to have to take a class than right after lunch. There is no blood leftover from the digestion process to go to your head and actually make it work. And when you have a history teacher that has been teaching the one o'clock slot for years because his delivery matched the time slot, you've got a real recipe for disaster.

Our professor was a real nice guy, but his delivery of the material was designed to aid in the sleep and digestion department. We had a class of about 120 students. History majors had dibs on the front seats, and then it was alphabetical from front to back down each row. I sat, alphabetically, about halfway back in the middle, which is too far back for my type to get anything from a class which doubles as a sleep aid.

The professor would look down at his lectern, simply reading the material. Every so often, not at any regular intervals, mind you, he would stop, look up, and smile. Then he would look back to the lectern and proceed in his best monotone.

So this is what I got. "In the year, humahumahum, there was humahum, blah blah blah humahumahuma." Pause. Look up. Smile. Look back down. "Furthermore, they wanted to hummmmmahummma ...." Snore. And my grade reflected my rapt attention.

I woke up one day in the middle of class to make an accidental discovery. My arousal from slumber inadvertently coincided with one of his "pause and smile" points. I accidentally happened to hear what he said just prior to the smile and realized that it was a humorous statement. Well, as humorous as history can be under the circumstances. I was jazzed. To think—each time he smiled, he was spewing forth historical humor, and I was missing it.

I woke up several of my friends around me to share my discovery. "Hey, you know when he smiles?" I asked.

"Yeah, so?"

"Well, every time he smiles, he's just told a joke!"

"No way!"

"Way! Just watch." I now had about twelve in my immediate area watching and trying to listen intently. Suddenly he looked up and grinned. Somehow we had missed it.

"Excuse me, sir," my friend Rick now had his hand in the air, "could you repeat that last line?"

The professor looked truly pleased for any sign of life and was only too happy to oblige. He reread the line, and it was, indeed, somewhat humorous. Of course, we all burst into laughter, and again, looking intensely pleased, he made a note in the margin. I think it must have been, "This is a very funny joke. Pause longer, smile broader."

His notes were so old they were yellow, and one day, as he turned the page, the page actually broke off. It was the first time anyone ever heard him say anything in class that wasn't scripted. I didn't actually see it break, but those who did described it as a scene of extreme frustration and bewilderment. He had flipped the page and the papyrus had actually broken. (OK, it wasn't papyrus, but it had to be the first run right after they discovered paper.) Anyway, he couldn't figure out what to do. A horrified look crossed his face, and the awkwardly long pause is what woke me up.

His notes were so old they were yellow, and one day, as he turned the page, the page actually broke off.

I woke up to actually hear him utter his now infamous, unscripted statement.

"Hmmmmmm," he said. Just like that. "Hmmmmmmm." Then he continued, "Guess I'll have to retype that page. (Yes, boys and girls, this was back in the day before computers, when every page had to be re-typed, not just reprinted.)

At any rate, he abruptly went on with the lecture, and I went into warped-mind mode. A few days earlier I had discovered a little door at the back of a mechanical closet in the student center. Being the curious sort, I opened it to see where it went. Well, as luck would have it, it didn't go anywhere, it just sat in its frame and swung back and forth. But on the other side of the door, I made a grand discovery. The little door was actually an access door to the space above the college dining hall. Not having time to do anything with this new information at the time, I had closed the little door and gone on my merry way.

Now, in the middle of history, my mind began to formulate a plan. Wouldn't it be cool to somehow tie on to a beam up there, open one of the ceiling tiles, and rappel down to lunch? Oh, that *would* be cool! But I would need help.

My friend Ronnie, quietly slumbering two rows over, was well known for his mountain climbing skills. He had all sorts of equipment. He would be a great choice for a partner on this escapade. I hastily wrote a note describing my discovery and my idea and passed it to Rick, sitting next to me, to pass over to Ron. Rick quickly scanned the note and then passed it on, while leaning back my direction to let me know that he wanted in on the gig too!

As soon as class was over, we headed for the student center. We slipped into the closet and swung open the magical access door. Wonderment and glee played on Ronnie and Rick's faces as we eased out onto the catwalk above the dining hall ceiling. It was a whole huge room by itself. Ronnie quickly located a beam above the ceiling grid that would work, and we lifted one corner of the tile to see where we would be in the dining hall. Perfect. We would drop right into the front left corner closest to the tray return. There was an exit nearby, so we could make our grand entrance and then, if necessary, beat a hasty retreat.

We decided since the next day was Thursday, and as such, there was chapel just before lunch, we would all take a chapel skip and set up while everyone else was in chapel.

Then, after chapel let out, the dining hall would fill up quickly with the post-chapel rush. We would wait until it got fairly full, and then make our big appearance.

That Thursday we worked the plan. Ronnie showed up with all of his gear. He'd even gone so far as to put his little German leather knickers and lederhosen on, to give it the alpine flair. We checked to make sure no one was looking and then ducked into the mechanical room. Once inside the attic of the dining hall, Ronnie located the right spot again and slipped a piece of webbing over the top of the beam and brought it back through, tying it off to make a loop.

Next, he tied the rope to the webbing and then pulled seat harnesses out of his climbing pack. After giving each of us one, he showed us how to put them on and how to clip in and went over safety procedures. We became aware of the cafeteria starting to buzz below us.

Chapel was out, and the rush was on. We had told no one of our plan, except my roommate Keith, so he could take pictures of the big event. We waited until the noise below us grew very lively, and then Ronnie stooped down and picked up the tile, moving it out of the way.

"You're first, Keele," Ronnie said. "This was your idea, so go for it."

"What do I do? What do I say?" I stammered, suddenly thinking maybe this was not such a good idea.

"Just clip in and go. As far as what to say ... say something witty like you always do, and we'll build on it when we come down," Ronnie said as he dropped the rope through the hole in the ceiling.

A hush suddenly fell on the crowd, and Ronnie clipped me in. I swung off the catwalk over the hole and began my descent. I got about halfway down and stopped as I looked all around the dining room. About a thousand people were staring back at me. I looked back up toward my comrades. Rick gave me the thumbs up sign and grinned.

"We should have turned left instead of right back there, guys!" I said, still looking up. The crowd roared. I slid on down the rope and landed right beside the academic dean who stood holding a tray waiting for me at the bottom of the rope. How had I missed seeing him before now?

"Keele," asked the dean, "does your mother know you're out doing stuff like this?"

"Um, no sir," I said, "and it would probably be best if you didn't tell her either."

He laughed *and walked away!* I was to later find out that he thought this was some sort of SA announcement and that I had asked permission from Mr. Evans, the cafeteria director. I looked around, and there was Mr. Evans, who naturally assumed since the dean was laughing and walking away, I must have asked permission from the dean. So he turned and went back into the kitchen.

Rick was next. He came down about halfway and stopped. "Whoa, we should have gone over a lot further!" He said. Again the crowd laughed.

He came on down as I said, "No, I think we should have turned left instead of right back there."

"No, we should have gone over farther!" he countered.

"Let's see what Ronnie thinks!" I said. "Hey, Ronnie!"

"Yeah?"

"Come on out and give us your opinion."

"Ok, just a second," came the voice from the attic.

I told you that Ronnie was wearing the little German leather knickers and lederhosen. What I didn't tell you is that Ronnie decided to really look the part, so he had put on his climbing pack with an ice axe and crampons and ropes all on the outside of it. He had so much stuff on that his ice axe got stuck in the ceiling as he tried to come through it. Ronnie had to pull himself back up with one hand and free his ice axe with the other, then turn and wiggle his way through the hole in the ceiling. Once free of the ceiling, he slid down about halfway.

"Hey—this ain't the girls dorm!" The crowd roared its delight yet again.

"I told you we should have turned left instead of right!"

"No, we should have gone over farther."

"You guys said we'd be in the girl's dorm." We went around and around with our lines as we walked out the nearby exit.

For months people stopped me and asked why we did it. "To bring a smile to someone's face, and to let them know that you can have fun as a Christian" was my only answer.

Some would just laugh and walk away. Others would walk away shaking their heads muttering about reprobates. Still others would simply make a statement about how Christians should act, implying that our behavior wasn't truly representative.

Let me ask you a question: Do you think God loved me any less at the bottom of the rope than He did at the top?

Somehow we've gotten the idea that God the Father is sitting on His throne, as humorist Ken Davis portrays Him, saying, "My people are having fun. NO!" as he stomps on the ground.

I think Ken is right when he said in his video *A Twisted Mind*: "What God is probably really saying is: 'Hey angels, come look at this idiot. Ah, I love this guy!'"

See, what I've learned since being cornered by a cane and halitosis is that God isn't stuffy at all. God loves me, warped ideas and all. God loves you, too, which brings me to my next point.

Point #4 – God's vision for me: Life as He lives it.
When you're the most Creative Person in the universe, how could He settle for a boring, drab life? God is concerned with the quality of human life.

John wrote, "I pray that you may enjoy good health and that all may go well with you, even as your soul is getting along well" (3 John 2).

God wants you to enjoy life. Maybe not slide down a rope into the dining hall, but truly enjoy life. Too many of us slip into a humdrum life of just going through the motions. We go to school, go to work, go home, go to bed. And in between, we seek to fill our days with artificial things, the glitz and glamor of this world. And we wonder where the joy is.

While that may be OK for a little while, God has much bigger plans for us. Check out one of my favorite texts in all of scripture. "'For I know the plans I have for you,' declares the Lord, 'plans to prosper you and not to harm you, plans to give you a hope and a future'" (Jer. 29:11).

God cares about your life! He cares about how you live it, because He wants you to get the most from it that you can. Don't use the line "you only go around once" as an excuse to throw your life away. God's vision for you is life as HE lives it. Full. Abundant. Exciting. Creative. Adventurous. Free of guilt, shame, and despair. He wants you to have a quality life—to have LIFE as He lives it.

Story #5 – *The Big Dark Woods*

I was five years old and I was ticked. My older sister had pushed me too far this time, and I decided it was time to get away from her and head out on my own. So I packed my car and left. OK, I put my favorite hot wheels into my pocket and went out the door. Same difference.

I marched across our big backyard, looked both ways at the road that came behind our place, marched across it, and then headed across the big field and down the hill into the big, dark woods. Usually the big, dark woods were not a place I would go to play by myself. But this day was different. I was angry and I didn't care. So I marched my little five-year-old self right into them. Down the big hill I went and came abruptly to the big creek. It was a bit big for me to cross, but no matter. I would turn and walk along it. Anywhere just to be free from *her*.

I hadn't noticed that it was getting close to dark, because I was mad. Have you noticed that when you're mad, you tend to miss important things like that? So there I was, ticked off and marching upstream along the creek with the sun going down. I pushed on through the briars and the thickets, thinking five-year-old angry thoughts.

"Who needs her anyway?" I muttered. "Well, I'm five years old, and I can take care of myself! I'm never going back! Never. Never. Never! I'll live out in the woods like Swift

Arrow. Only I won't live with the Indians. Just out in the woods. I'll learn to swing from tree to tree and everything." On and on I went for some time.

When I finally noticed the lengthening shadows and the deepening darkness, I reasoned that I *could* live in the woods a bit closer to home. I would still be in the woods, but closer to home, you know, just in case. So I turned around and headed back down the creek bank the way I had previously come. Only now, I wasn't quite as mad, and I was starting to get a little bit scared.

In the part of the country where we lived at the time, there were coyotes that roamed quite freely. Usually, after dark. In my five-year-old anger, I had also forgotten about them. Now somewhere behind me, farther upstream, I got a chilling reminder.

AHHOOOOOOOOOOW, came a coyote howl. The little hairs on the back of my neck stood on end. I was a little less angry and a little more scared. I picked up the pace as I pushed back through the briars and thickets I had come through earlier in my anger.

AHHHOOOOOOOOOOOOOOOOOOOOWWW! Came a response a little closer to where I was. I picked up the pace again. Not real angry anymore, but a whole lot scared. As I pushed on, my ears and my imagination began to hear everything that was and wasn't out there. I heard (or thought I heard) heavy, coyote breathing. I imagined the saliva dripping off of the long coyote fangs, just like the cartoon wolves looking at a flock of sheep, as the coyotes watched me with their night vision skills.

AAAAHHHHOOOOOOOOOOOOOOOOOOOWWWWW! A loud one came real close by. Forget the anger … I was now in a full-scale panic. My eyes bugged out, my heart raced, and I began clawing my way through the thickets, bouncing off of trees and yelling my little five-year-old lungs out.

"HELLLLLLLLLLLLLLLLLLLLLP!!!" I screamed as loud as I could. I bounced off the sixth tree before I heard a voice that was sweet music to my ears.

"Donnie! Dooooonnieeeeeeee! Where are you?" It was *DAD*! He was looking for me! "Donnie!"

"Over here!" I yelled as loud as I could.

"Keep talking, son!" Dad yelled back.

"Overhereoverhereoverhereoverhereoverhere!" I yelled, and soon I was scooped up into my dad's strong arms, and before long I found myself being carried out of the big, dark woods, across the meadow, across the road, across the big, backyard and into the safety of home.

Point #5 – There is in the heart of God a place I know as home. It doesn't matter how angry I get at my sister. It doesn't matter how far into the big, dark woods I go. It doesn't matter if the coyotes are coming. No matter how dark and scary my picture looks, if I listen, I can hear the voice of my Father calling. He's looking for me! He'll stride right into the middle of my dark and scary woods, even though my anger and my running is what caused the problem, and He'll pick me up and carry me back to the safety of home. There is in the heart of God a place I know as home.

And if I read scripture correctly, there is a place in the heart of God for you too!

John 6:37 says, "Whoever comes to me I will never drive away." Matthew 11:28 says, "Come to me, all you who are weary and burdened, and I will give you rest." And here's one of the best: "And surely I am with you always, to the very end of the age" (Matt. 28:20).

This world has become a dark and scary place to live. As the shadows of earth's history lengthen and the darkness deepens, we know that our enemy is on the prowl. The Bible doesn't compare him to a coyote, but to a roaring lion, looking for someone to devour (see 1 Peter 5:8). He's closing in because he knows his time is short.

You, like me, may be angry at a brother or a sister in the church. You may be running away from home. Running across the street into the big, dark woods. You may suddenly find yourself being tracked by a ferocious predator, and your hope is rapidly vanishing into a world that seems dark.

But stop. Stop running and listen. The Father is calling your name. He's looking for *you!* Like Adam, He's still asking you the same question. "Where are you?" And if you answer, He'll come and scoop you up into His big, strong arms and carry you back to the safety of HOME.

> **Stop running and listen. The Father is calling your name. He's looking for *you!***

There is in the Father's heart, a place that you can know as home. He's calling. Are you answering?

The Conclusion

What we've just done in the past five stories is completely shared a synopsis of all twenty-eight fundamental Adventist beliefs. Every one of our doctrines can be tied to one of these five points. Let's look at them again.

- Point #1 – The Bible is the Word of God—not a rule-book, but a roadmap.

- Point #2 – Jesus Christ is the One who never changes in a universe that always does.

- Point #3 – God keeps a family album, and my picture is in it.

- Point #4 –God's vision for me: Life as He lives it.

- Point #5 – There is in the heart of God a place I know as home.

Think of any doctrine, and see if you can tie it to one of those points. Not sure how that works. Let's look at a few examples. Are you worried about the judgment? Does it scare you? Check out point #3. God keeps a family album, and your picture is in it. That's exactly what the book of life is that Revelation talks about. It's God's family album. It's an album of all of His children—you and me.

What about a healthy lifestyle? I don't see that in there. Look closer. Point #4 – God's vision for me: Life as He lives it. For you and I to have an abundant and full life, it only makes sense to keep our bodies healthy.

OK. What about the second coming? That's a core Adventist belief. The soon imminent return of Jesus. Check out point #5. There is in the heart of God a place I know as home. Your Father has you in his heart. He's looking for you and has promised to come get you. Both now, in your day to day life, and when He comes again.

Get the idea? OK. Now you try it. Think of a doctrine and see which one of those five points it hits. Next time you think studying doctrines is boring, just remember roadmaps, rappelling, and the big, dark woods, and you'll have a good idea what you believe.

CHAPTER 9

A Patch of Sunshine

"Pastor Don, it's pouring down rain! How are we going to paint that lady's house today?"

What do you say to a group of teens who have just posed a very pertinent question?

It was the last full day of our mission trip in the mountains of Eastern Kentucky. The previous day we had worked on Barbara's house. Barbara had three children she was trying to raise on her own. Six years earlier, Barbara had returned to their small hillside shack after going to the store for her husband, only to find he had committed suicide while she was gone.

Living had been meager since then. It had also grown more violent. A friend of her late husband had decided that Barbara was going to be his woman whether she wanted to be or not. Whenever he got drunk and decided that he needed a woman, he would head up to the hillside shack and break down a door, or bust a window or even tear off boards from the side of the shack and break through the inner sheetrock and then brutally rape her as her three children cowered in one of the other rooms of the small house. Repeated calls to the police yielded no results since they "didn't really see nothin' happen, so how do we know ya ain't lyin'?" These episodes were repeated about two or three times per month.

Day one, we fixed a hole in her foundation that allowed the floor to droop downward away from the wall, leaving a gaping twelve-inch hole for the rats to run in and out at will. We re-roofed her sagging, leaking roof, and fixed her chimney and stovepipe to reduce the risk of this becoming a fire hazard. We re-floored her bedroom and patched sheetrock throughout the house. We painted the inside of the house and even fixed the bare-wired electrical outlets. We worked as hard as we could, but somehow, it seemed that every time we finished one project, there were two more that we still needed to do. We decided that we would have to come back and finish the exterior the next day. We would fix all of the holes on the exterior and broken windows and then paint the house.

I was up at 5:30 a.m. and looked outside. Rain. Pouring rain. Instantly, I panicked. How would we finish Barbara's house? A small voice reminded me that Jesus had controlled the storm on the lake, and if I would just trust, He could do it again. I relaxed and began my personal devotions. By the time I had finished reviewing the story in scripture, I was sure that God would work a miracle for us. During my prayer time, I asked God for a miracle.

I stepped out of my room and headed for the kitchen. One of the staff came into the dining area and informed me that the weatherman was calling for 100 percent chance of rain. So far, he was right. But the weatherman forgot to talk to my God about it. Each time a student asked me what we were going to do, I simply answered, "We are going to pray and ask God not to let the weather interfere with our work and then go for it."

They gave me *that* look that only teenagers can give. That look that says, "I think you'd be better off in a straight jacket," but simply shrugged their shoulders and just said, "OK, whatever."

At the close of worship, I asked everyone to join me in a prayer session where we claimed the promise found in

John 14:13, 14: "And I will do whatever you ask in my name, so that the Father may be glorified in the Son. You may ask me for anything in my name, and I will do it."

"Lord," I prayed, "You've given us Your promise, and we believe that we are doing Your will. Please don't let the rain interfere with our work. May we show Your love to Barbara and her family today. In Jesus name, Amen."

"All right, load up." We headed out the door into the pouring rain. The farther up the valley we drove, the harder it rained.

"Um, Pastor Don," one teen ventured, "it's still raining."

Without thinking, I shot back, "We're not there yet! He doesn't need for it to stop yet." We drove on in silence. Finally, we turned onto the little road that led up the hillside to Barbara's little shack. Amazingly, the higher we drove, the less it rained, until we finally turned off into her little driveway. Just a mist now. "All right, guys," I said, "God's done His part, let's do ours!" By the time we finished unloading ladders and tools, the sun was beginning to peek out. Our whole group was pumped! God had performed a miracle just for us!

It was about an hour later as I finished pounding a nail into some siding that I happened to look off the side of the mountain down to the main road that wound through the little town of Pineville, Kentucky. It was then that I realized that we had a bigger miracle than we had at first realized. I called the whole group together.

"Look down there. What do you see?" I asked.

"Why, it's raining hard down there," someone exclaimed. "Look, you can even see trucks and cars with their windshield wipers going."

Another joined in, "Look, it's raining so hard down there that the road almost looks white!"

"Hey guys, look over there to the left," someone else exclaimed.

Another yelled, "Hey, look to the right."

Everyone spun around to look behind us up over the mountain.

We were under God's umbrella as we stood there in that little patch of bright sunshine.

Sure enough. Rain. We had rain on every side! We were under God's umbrella as we stood there in that little patch of bright sunshine looking 500 yards in every direction at the pouring rain.

John 14:13, 14 still rings true today: "And I will do whatever you ask in my name, so that the Father may be glorified in the Son. You may ask me for anything in my name, and I will do it."

CHAPTER 10

Vending Machine God

"If you let Dad die, God, I'll quit the ministry," I muttered to myself as I sped down I-205 toward my parent's house in Portland, Oregon. Up to this point, my life had been one of pleasant memories, successful youth ministry, and happy times with my family. To be sure, we had our moments, but now, suddenly I was faced with one of the most difficult situations of my life. We had watched as a rather large lump under dad's right arm had turned into an ugly, oozing, bleeding, ulcerous tumor that was approximately seven to nine inches across. The diagnosis: melanoma, the worst form of skin cancer. The prognosis: three to six months.

We prayed. We wept. We encouraged others to pray with us. Thousands from all across the country, even across the world, prayed that my dad would be healed. I felt sure that healing was in the bag. If it had to do with the amount of prayers or the sincerity of prayer, then my dad should have been healed. If it had to do with faith and seeking the Lord, then my dad should have been healed. But he wasn't. He died.

A few Sundays before Dad died, he could not stand up without two or three people helping him out of bed. I had spent the greater portion of the night praying. I really wanted God to work a miracle. I had read the stories in the gospels of all the people Jesus healed. I had read the stories in Acts where Peter (Acts 5:15, 16) was walking through crowds and people were clamoring to put their sick in his shadow as they passed and they were healed. I had read stories of Paul (Acts 19:11, 12) walking through crowds who were passing their handkerchiefs and aprons over to Paul so that he might touch them and send them back, and Acts declares that all of them were healed.

Then there were the proclamations of Jesus, "If you believe, you will receive whatever you ask for in prayer" (Matt. 21:22). "Ask and it will be given to you; seek and you will find; knock and the door will be opened to you" (Matt. 7:7). "So that whatever you ask in my name the Father will give you" (John 15:16).

I believed. I had asked. I didn't doubt that God could do it. I had prayed hard and long that night, yet somehow, I was still like the disciples in the Garden of Gethsemane. Somewhere along the line, I had fallen asleep. Now doubt plagued me. Would my sleeping preclude my miracle? Never mind that I had only averaged three to four hours of sleep for the previous three weeks as I sat by the bedside of my dying father. Never mind that I was driving forty minutes one way to go home at least once during each twenty-four hour period and see my family, and that, usually for only an hour or two. This particular night I had decided I would keep a prayer vigil and pray all night. Yet, I found myself waking up on the floor of my study at 4:00 a.m. loathing the weakness of my humanity. "Lord, I believe!" I cried, "Help my unbelief!"

About six o'clock, I felt an impression to go to Dad's and say to him, "In the name of Jesus Christ of Nazareth, rise up and be healed." And so now I sped down I-205 wrestling with myself and God. The struggle raged. Inwardly, I said, "If I go and do this thing, and nothing happens, I'll be really embarrassed. How would that look for a pastor?" On the other hand, I thought, "But if I don't, that could be the very thing that saves him." I thought of Naaman's servant saying, "If he had asked you to do a big thing, wouldn't you have done it?" I wrestled. I prayed. And then the thought came, "If you let Dad die, God, I'll quit the ministry." The turmoil continued to rage for most of the trip. As I turned into Dad's neighborhood, a peace overtook me, and I was resolute that God wanted me to go in and pray and ask Him to raise Dad up. I was confident that God would do that.

I entered the room. No one was with Dad at the time, so I told him that I felt impressed that we should pray for his healing once again, only this time, I felt that God was calling on us to demonstrate our faith in Him by actions. Dad said, "I think you are right. I appreciate that about you ... always being a man of faith."

I prayed. Hard. And then I said, "In the name of Jesus Christ, I say to you, get up and be healed." Without hesitation, Dad, holding on to my hand, swung his feet off the bed and began to feebly stand. About halfway up, he gathered strength from somewhere and straightened all the way up. We both stood there holding on to each other for a magical moment wondering if indeed the healing was happening, and then he said, "Help me lay back down. God may heal me in stages." I helped him back into bed and then he said, "Thanks for your faith. Thanks for your love that would prompt you to pray for me. And don't worry. God will heal me. Now or then."

> **I prayed. Hard. And then I said, "In the name of Jesus Christ, I say to you, get up and be healed."**

I left the room very bewildered, very embarrassed, and very angry. Angry with God for asking me to do that. Angry with myself for possibly misreading His cues. Angry because it felt as if the devil was just taunting me, throwing my faith in my face as totally preposterous. Was it a lack of faith? Was I acting on what I believed God wanted me to do? Why would God have me pray a prayer that He wasn't going to answer?

I don't think Dad ever mentioned it again, and I wondered if he was embarrassed by it. He didn't seem to be. The thing that got me was that his trust was immediate. He was willing to try whatever means were available because he loved us and he loved life so much. And he truly believed that God was going to heal him. So to him, I don't think he was embarrassed, even though I was.

After much thought, here is what I think the point must be—or at least some thoughts that can be drawn from the whole experience. First, I think that God may have been testing me to see if I would trust Him no matter what. I had thought that if Dad died, I would leave the ministry. What use would it be to serve a God who didn't answer prayers? Why minister to the goodness of a God that wasn't so good? I think God's point was, "Hey, no matter what happens, I will still be in control and you don't have to worry. I will take care of your dad. And I will take care of you. So do you believe me or not?"

Second, I would have regretted never trying it if I had kept silent and Dad had died. I could truly say that I had tried everything, and I could rest knowing that God had another plan. If I had never experienced that, I could never have forgiven myself, and so I think God gave me the urge to go ahead and try what I had read in the Bible. I think God wanted me to see that sometimes all of the notions that we have, or all of the "magic" words we want to speak do not hold the power. Only God does. I figured that if those words worked in the Bible, they just might work now, and that if I didn't try them, they might have been the words to save Dad. But such is not the case.

God is not moved by my "magic" words. He is moved by my heart. He isn't interested in my notions. What He wants is to be loved freely. With no strings attached. With no "magic" words. And He risks being misunderstood and spurned rather than perform to my tune. The love He wants me to share with Him is not a love based on manipulation or insecurity. It is a love based on a deep abiding trust. And the question comes back, "Do I trust Him no matter what?" If I only trust Him when things are going my way, then I have a conditional love. If I only trust Him when He responds to my "magic" words, then I have reduced Him to a vending machine God—put in the right amount, say the "magic" words, and out will pop my desired outcome. That's not a relationship. It's manipulation.

When I say to God, "do this and I will love you" or "don't do this and I will not love You," I am basing my relationship on my own immature desire to manipulate Him to get what I want. God has never worked that way, not even when it would have saved Jesus' life. Herod wanted Jesus to perform a miracle in exchange for Jesus' freedom. He didn't yield because He wanted our love to be from a genuine response to His love, not from a manipulated response based on what we might get.

And so, I am finding a deeper relationship with God, even though Dad died. Even though healing didn't occur the way I wanted. Why? Because I can't blame God for all of the misery ... we chose it. WE sinned, not God. "But God demonstrates his love for us in this: While we were still sinners, Christ died for us" (Rom. 5:8).

Love only wants a genuine response. So Love stretched out His arms and died. To show us He loved us. To show us that though the devil has made death to be a fearful thing, we need not fear it. To show us that He understands even the worst of what happens to us, and yet has promised us a better day. And because of that promise, I still have something to share in the ministry. And because of that love, I'll stay in the ministry until that day. A day when all will be made right. A day when we will see why things didn't work out here. A day for joy instead of tears. And a day when Dad will be raised up.

We invite you to view the complete
selection of titles we publish at:

www.TEACHServices.com

Scan with your mobile
device to go directly
to our website.

Please write or email us your praises, reactions, or
thoughts about this or any other book we publish at:

TEACH Services, Inc.
P U B L I S H I N G
www.TEACHServices.com • (800) 367-1844

info@TEACHServices.com

TEACH Services, Inc., titles may be purchased in bulk for
educational, business, fund-raising, or sales promotional use.
For information, please e-mail:

BulkSales@TEACHServices.com

Finally, if you are interested in seeing
your own book in print, please contact us at

publishing@TEACHServices.com

We would be happy to review your manuscript for free.